Godfoolery

Is he willing to prevent evil, but not able?
Then he is impotent.
Is he able, but not willing?
Then he is malevolent.
Is he both able and willing?
Whence then is evil?[1]

---

1. The alleged question posed by Epicurus 341–270 BCE as formulated by David Hume in *Dialogues Concerning Natural Religion*, 75.

Godfoolery

Beyond Belief and Unbelief

JOHN FULLING CROSBY

Preface by Rev. Barbara Carlson

WIPF & STOCK · Eugene, Oregon

GODFOOLERY
Beyond Belief and Unbelief

Copyright © 2022 John Fulling Crosby. All rights reserved. Except for brief quotations in critical publications or reviews, no part of this book may be reproduced in any manner without prior written permission from the publisher. Write: Permissions, Wipf and Stock Publishers, 199 W. 8th Ave., Suite 3, Eugene, OR 97401.

Wipf & Stock
An Imprint of Wipf and Stock Publishers
199 W. 8th Ave., Suite 3
Eugene, OR 97401

www.wipfandstock.com

PAPERBACK ISBN: 978-1-6667-4479-8
HARDCOVER ISBN: 978-1-6667-4480-4
EBOOK ISBN: 978-1-6667-4481-1

Contents

Preface vii

Introduction ix

Chapter 1: Are We *Ex Nihilo*? 1

Chapter 2: Abortion 5

Chapter 3: The Social Gospel of Jesus and Modern Socialism 9

Chapter 4: Genesis: Atonement Theology as Godfoolery 12

Chapter 5: O Death, Where is Thy Victory? 18

Chapter 6: You Won't Be Disappointed 20

Chapter 7: Theodicy: Making Excuses for God and Explaining and Defending the God Hypothesis 23

Chapter 8: Four Strikes and You're Out 26

Chapter 9: Tribalism and White Supremacy 31

Chapter 10: Bible Stories Not Learned in Sunday School: Onan and the Death Penalty for *Coitus Interruptus* 42

Chapter 11: Bible Stories Not Learned in Sunday School: King David Has His Way with Bathsheba and Then Arranges for Her Husband to Be Killed in Battle 46

Chapter 12: Whose Reality is True? Tests of Truth 49

Chapter 13: So You Want to Study the Bible! Let's Begin with the Higher and Lower Criticism 54

Chapter 14: Credulous and Incredulous 59

Chapter 15: Death: An Existential Paradox 68

Bibliography 77

OTHER BOOKS BY JOHN F. CROSBY

Witness For Christ. Westminster, 1965.
From Religion To Grace: Thinking Through the Doctrine of Justification by Faith. Abingdon, 1967.
Illusion and Disillusion: The Self In Love and Marriage. Wadsworth, 1973, 1975, 1985, 1981.
Sexual Autonomy: Toward A humanistic Ethic. Charles C. Thomas, 1981.
Choice and Challenge: Contemporary Readings In Marriage. Co-editor with Carl Williams. W. C. Brown, 1974.
Choice and Challenge: Contemporary Readings In Marriage. Co-editor with Carl Williams. W. C. Brown, 1979.
Reply To Myth: Perspectives On Intimacy. Editor. John Wylie and Sons, 1985.
When One Wants Out and the Other Doesn't. Editor. Brunner/Mazel, 1989.
Grounds For Marriage: If Only I Had Known. AuthorHouse, 2005.
If Only I Had Listened: Grounds For Marrige II. Authorhouse, 2019.
Aftermath: Surviving the Loss of God. Algora, 2013.
Sons and Fathers. Routledge, 2014.
Grounds For Marriage II; If Only I Had Listened. AuthorHouse, 2019.
Divided We Stood: A Tale of the Lost Orders. Holon, 2015.
The Flipside of Godspeak: Theism As Constructed Reality. Wipf and Stock, 2007.
Faithlore: The Invented Reality. Wipf and Stock, 2018.

Preface

INTEGRITY OF LIFE IS John Crosby's gift to the reader.

After completing theological studies at Princeton Theological Seminary, and following the path of his devout Presbyterian parents for eleven years, John realized he could no longer speak assuring words of eternal life at a graveside service. Godfoolery words based on a biblical story of prehistory when Eve ate the fruit of the Tree and enticed Adam to eat, bringing down on Eve centuries of blame for bringing sin into the world.

John's wife, Marjorie, stood by him faithfully. She enrolled in advanced studies to become a Nurse Midwife. Together, they raised three sons, each successful in their chosen professions

John's parents, especially his mother, were deeply disappointed in his resignation from ministry. When he chose to obtain an advanced degree in Marriage and Family Studies and became a professor at Indiana University and the University of Kentucky, as well as a successful author on marriage preparation, raising healthy children, and father-son relationships, his mother was proud.

Human beings have organized themselves in tribes throughout centuries. The tribes of Israel are an example of a people who in captivity in Egypt did not assimilate but remained a distinct tribe. Current positive tribes include Quakers, Amish, Mennonites, and Mormons.

In early writings Lincoln supported African American freedom. but Andrew Johnson who became President after Lincoln's assassination did not. When Andrew Jackson became

Preface

President he sent Cherokees on a trail of tears from their native homeland to regions west of the Mississippi River. Other Indian tribes suffered a similar fate.

In our time former President Donald J Trump has created a cult of Trumpism. Several Republican Senators, Representatives, and political appointees wanted to be part of his demented tribe "wherein there is no tolerance for dissent. Truth be damned." The Trump tribe actively seeks to prevent progressive voters and people of color from voting and endeavors to disenfranchise them in a destructive bed of racism and white supremacy.

In the final chapter Dr. Crosby notes that death is an essential paradox integral to the meaning of life, yet also the final exit point.

Crosby cites Viktor Frankl, a psychiatrist who survived the brutalities of Auschwitz as a monument to the power of the human brain to persist in the midst of total chaos.

Life ultimately means the responsibility to find the right answer to its problems and the fulfillment of tasks which it constantly sets for each individual.

Am I my brother's and sister's keeper? If so, what is required of me now?

The Rev. Barbara Carlson,
M. Div., Starr King, Berkeley

Introduction

THIS IS A SMALL volume of essays. Each essay can stand by itself or can be tied in with other thoughts. Not too many of us have the opportunity to put in writing the reasons for some of the important events and decisions in their life. I am fortunate in that I have this wonderful opportunity.

Not all these thoughts are new. Certainly they are not original. I refer to my previous publications on this subject: *Aftermath: Surviving the Loss of God; The Flipside of Godspeak: Theism As Constructed Reality;* and *Faithlore: The Invented Reality.* I stand by *Sons and Fathers: Challenges To Paternal Authority* as a definitive work on the importance of family on early childhood.

I am most appreciative of the support I have received from fellow agnostics and skeptics amongst my fellow Unitarian Universalists, especially the Humanists and the Freethinkers plus my breakfast geezers (once a week breakfast since 2006) served as support and encouragement. We continued on Zoom throughout the COVID-19 pandemic. I am also appreciative of Starr King graduate and Unitarian minister, Barbara Carlson, who penned the preface.

I was hospitalized during November and December of 2020 and have recovered. Marjorie and I were married sixty-five years before she succumbed to pneumonia and COVID-19. Even though I had told her my "book-writing days" were over, I could not separate these essays from my drive to write. I dedicate this work to Marjorie inasmuch as she concurred with almost all of my thinking.

INTRODUCTION

All names are, of course, fictitious, but the circumstances and dynamics of the four "strikes" of Chapter Eight are still very much alive in my mind's eye. I still love and grieve each of them.

John Fulling Crosby

CHAPTER ONE

Are We *Ex Nihilo*?

IF YOU REALLY BELIEVE in God, the theistic God of the New Testament, the Old Testament, the Koran, and the Talmud, then you might be well-advised to put this book down. Don't read one sentence further. It is loaded with stuff you definitely do not want to hear. Certainly, it will not be good for your health.

In the third grade, or was it fourth grade, my teacher scolded me harshly for my tomfoolery. I have no idea what I had done or what I had said. But she said I was doing tomfoolery! I knew I would catch hell from my mother because somehow things like this traveled home fast, even without the internet or a smart phone. I feared that my dad, when he got home from work, would get on my case and ask me what he should tell the neighbors and the people at church. I just shrugged the whole thing off.

I didn't know who or what "tomfoolery" was. Today, my *Webster's New World* tells me tomfoolery is practiced by a tomfool. That's not much help! Today's dictionary tells me: "... poor Tom formerly applied to the demented and retarded, a foolish, stupid, or silly person. adj. foolish, stupid, or silly. Tomfoolery is foolish behavior; silliness; nonsense.[1] For me it was a small step from tomfoolery to Godfoolery.

Godfoolery, then, is our human preoccupation with inventing and creating, and continuing to invent and create, the

---

1. *Webster's New World Dictionary*, s.v. "Tomfoolery."

godhead, that is, the theistic founder and creator and sustainer of all existence, from the lowly insect to the most gigantic whale, hippopotamus, great white shark, or dinosaur—from the planets of the solar system to the outer reaches of space, amongst millions of galaxies, black holes, and novas.

What we cannot understand we create. What we do not comprehend we devise according to our own imagination and specification. And then (this is the kicker) we actually believe or trust in what we create.

Godfoolery is the human preoccupation with creating or inventing god and then proscribing and prescribing the dictates we imagine this god requires of us.

This all started with me somewhere in the early years when I attended the Presbyterian church. I guess I absorbed a lot of "lore" about god and life and theology.[2]

Nevertheless, we are the foolish ones. We who believe that there actually is a Creator god/force are the nonsensical ones. We are called theists in contradiction to deists who believe there is a creator god who is transcendent, i.e. distant and all-powerful in terms of creating and setting the universe(s) in motion (the watchmaker analogy). This is often referred to as "creation ex-nihilo" or creation out of nothing.

I have a philosophy book that claims it is a grave error in our thinking about god to ask the logical questions: "Where did god come from?" or "Who or what made god?"[3] To many people, this is a second or third grade question. Nevertheless, I am in my ninetieth year and I am still asking it. Sahakian and Sahakian, among others in the philosophical/legalistic tradition, claim that the question of who or what made god is a logical fallacy, or contradiction, since it assumes that god made god (logical fallacy). If we accept this argument it would then be impossible to take any philosophical stance because the argument from cause to effect would, in itself, be a logical contradiction or a logical fallacy. It would be kicking the can further down the road. To accept that

---

2. Crosby, *Faithlore*. Also see: *Flipside of Godspeak*.
3. Sahakian and Sahakian, *Ideas of the Great Philosophers*, 20, 103.

there is some form of "god above god" (as Paul Tillich has done) would become a new item of faith. To insist that there is some sort of deistic/creator puts us right back into the hotbed of religious faith. On this point, there is little difference between theists and deists.

Freud's take on religious belief

I think Sigmund Freud's "The Future of an Illusion" comes closest to answering the question as to why belief in some sort of divine theistic force has endured, especially in western civilization.[4] Quite simply, we are born into a relationship of total dependency upon our mother. Without mother we will not survive. To survive we would need incubation, tons of TLC, and nutrition from a lactating mother or mother-substitute.

Freud's main point is that as we navigate the early months and years we come to sense that our security also depends on a father who protects both me and my mother. We don't realize what's going on as we continue to grow up. A massive transference takes place wherein our primal parental dependency is transferred to an all-supportive heavenly father. Sidebar 1 describes the process.

In contrast to Freud, psychoanalyst Melanie Klein talks about the good breast and the bad breast. Klein centers her theory on the mother-child relationship while Freud is preoccupied with the father-son relationship. Klein heralds the advent of splitting and projection wherein every negative thought or emotion is thrust outward upon others and every positive thought or emotion is internalized. According to Klein the first four weeks of life are the most telling and crucial for all later development.[5]

---

4. Freud, *Future of an Illusion*, 47.

5. As Quoted from Etherington, "Melanie Klein and Object Relations Theory."

> **SIDEBAR 1**
>
> ...The terrifying impression of helplessness in childhood around the need for protection—for protection through love—which was provided by the father; and the recognition that this helplessness lasts throughout life made it necessary to cling to the existence of a father, but this time a more powerful one. Thus the benevolent rule of a divine Providence allays our fear of the dangers of life; the establishment of a moral world order ensures the fulfillment of the demands of justice...and the prolongation of earthly existence in a future life provides the local and temporal framework in which these wish-fulfillments shall take place.1
>
> 1. Freud, *Future of an Illusion*, 46.

Jump Ahead to John Calvin

Calvin once claimed that the human brain was a "perpetual forge of idols."[6] Calvin was concerned with physical images rather than mental constructions. I counter Calvin because I claim that all god talk is a form of psychological constructivism. We create god. More precisely, we invent god.[7] I go even further: to me, all religious belief and doctrine throughout history and in every continent and nationality is *lore*.

---

6. Calvin, *Institutes of the Christian Religion*, 97. "The impiety of attributing a visible form to God. The setting up of idols a defection from the true God." Based on Gen 31:19.

7. Crosby, *Faithlore*. Also: *Flipside of Godspeak*.

Chapter Two

Abortion

Let's all be clear about one thing. In all theistic belief systems it is the belief in the reputed, revealed, or established god that forms the backbone for belief in anti-abortion. This belief is at the heart of the so-called Trump base that gave Trump his rigid and unyielding fundamentalist base. Trump declared himself against abortion. This single Trumpian belief provided the basis for four years of Trump being forgiven for sexual escapades, including the so-called "Hollywood Access" tape wherein Trump bragged about his sexual license to intrude privately upon women if he deemed them as being of his type.

As of October of 2020, President Trump took no responsibility for the physical separation of nearly five hundred children who had been forcibly taken from their parents and were living in cages at the Mexican border. Trump said it was all right because his predecessor, Barack Obama, had built the cages.

The issue of abortion will *never* be solved or resolved on the basis of theology. Or philosophy. Individual humans have to figure this one out for themselves. At heart, however, are two questions of great importance.

1. When does human life begin? Not just life, because surely the three hundred mullion sperm in a single human male ejaculation are alive. And surely the lifetime supply of ovarian eggs-in-waiting are alive within the female. The question,

historically and physiologically, is when does *human* life begin.[1] This question is answerable. I believe human life begins the instant a neonate is able to survive on its own without the aid of incubator, breathing apparatus, or other life-preserving devices.

2. When, and under what conditions and circumstances, does one branch of government, faction, group, tribe or, cult have the right to prescribe or proscribe when, if ever, a pregnant human female, married or unmarried, may elect to undergo an abortive procedure? This second question is specific and answerable. This right is the exclusive right of the birth mother. No court, judiciary, legislature, theological body, or executive of whatever stripe or description has the exclusive and inherent right of the birth mother.

Historial Overview

Our society exhibits a strong resistance to history and to the practices of past time. Abortion has been practiced since antiquity. Greece and Rome, even in the environs of the early Christian world, practiced abortion. The Romans also practiced infanticide. As recently as 1800, none of the then United States had laws prohibiting abortion. By 1900, however, the scene had shifted to the viewpoint that considered abortion to be a criminal offense. In the early nineteenth century, the controlling mode of thought was the concept of the quickening, the first movement of the fetus within the uterus. ... The English common law held that destruction of the fetus prior to quickening was not an offense. In 1800, a quickened fetus was still not considered to be a human life...In the United States, abortion prior to quickening was not considered illegal until many years later.... Increasingly, through the decades following the 1850's the medical profession opposed the practice of abortion. It was mainly due to their efforts that legislation against

1. Crosby, "When Does Human Life Begin?"

abortion came about. The American Medical Association considered a disruption of pregnancy at any point to be a crime.²

Hardin reframes the issue from abortion to compulsory pregnancy. Hardin's argument, and those of Jaggar and Thompson are examples of functionalist-utilitarian thought favoring abortion. Rahmeier and Brody provide examples of the philosophical literature that comes to grips with the specific issue of the point at which life begins.³

Population and Global Economics

However, the real reason abortion must always remain a viable and legal option stems from the stark reality of world population and the related questions of food supply and economic viability. Simply put, how much population can earth support? Food supply and the ability to earn money or other medium of exchange will eventually overpower all theological, philosophical, or moral arguments in favor of making abortion illegal.

In conclusion, we must face the facts that religion, on the whole, especially evangelical and fundamentalist religious persuasions, consider abortion as wrong, sinful, and the work of the devil. Nevertheless in the Old Testament and in Talmudic writings of the Jewish Torah, we note that life is cheap and that warfare was acceptable (to the Talmudic Jew adultery was defined as sexual intercourse with another Jewish man's wife.)

2. Crosby, "When Does Human Life Begin?" 356–57.
3. Hardin, "Abortion or compulsory pregnancy?" 246; Jaggar, A. "A Woman's Right To Decide," 347–60; Thompson, "A defense of abortion," 47–66; Rahmeier, "Abortion and the reverence for life;" Brody, "Fetal humanity and the theory of essentials."

> *We have to consider the effect of a growing global population. According to UN predictions, global population will increase to nine billion by 2050, when it will stabilize and may even drop slightly. However, that means there will be a further two billion people on the planet in the next 35 years.) This is because as countries develop they go through a demographic transition .... Demographic tradition refers to the transition from high birth and death rates to low birth and death rates as a country develops from a pre-industrial to an industrialized economic system. However, infant and mother mortality rates are quick to drop as an area obtains better sanitation and health care provision. A societal shift to lower birth rates can take a long time, and it is during this time of transition that a large increase in population occurs. Globally, the highest increase in global population was in the 1960's with growth of over 2 percent per year due to the roll out of mass immunizations and the eradication of smallpox. The most effecctive solution to high birth rate has been the education of women up to at least secondary school level, as they take control of their own fertility... In general the greatest population increases are occurring in the least developed countries.*[1]

1. Maslin, *Climate Change*, 169–70.

I end this chapter on abortion by asking, "What would Jesus say?"

Who really knows? No one. But I end with a cautionary principle. In Jesus' name I would look at the whole familial scene. As a family therapist I would consider how the marital couple are handling the vicissitudes of life, income, employment, community standing, and contribution to communal life and the public welfare. If husband and wife cannot agree, the vote of the wife/mother must prevail.

CHAPTER THREE

The Social Gospel of Jesus and Modern Socialism

I GET VERY TIRED of the mantras ridiculing socialism. Hell, we had a president who appeared to be in bed with Putin's communistic autocracy and we allow our senate to whitewash him. Here are some questions:

Perhaps we should all go back to grade school or junior high school and re-study what capitalism and socialism are all about. Perhaps we should reread Plato's *Republic*.

Perhaps we should study the way our forefathers and horse trainers from ancient Persian and Alexandrian times have conspired to fashion the "bridal" assembly we attach to the horse's neck and mouth so that we can guide or steer the horse to the right or left. Much like the bridled horse, with a "bit" between its jaws, it is no shame to embrace a "bridled" capitalism, i.e. controlled and well-governed.

When I was a Presbyterian minister I was a social gospel type. In the early and mid-eighteen hundreds (post Civil War) there was a strong movement of fundamentalism throughout our country with emphasis on personal salvation, sin, hell, and damnation, heaven, and theories of atonement. Much of the so-called social gospel movement grew up in reaction to this fundamentalism.

A courageous minister by the name of Harry Emerson Fosdick became the most famous representative of what became

Protestant liberalism and the social gospel movement. You may even recall that the famous Riverside church in New York City was built so that Fosdick would have a centralized national pulpit.

Please read again, with diligence, the Sermon on the Mount: Matthew 5, 6, and 7. Then proceed to Matthew 25: 31–46 which here follows as a sidebar.

> When the son of man comes in his glory, and all the angels with him, then he will sit on his glorious throne. Before him will be gathered all the nations, and he will separate them one from the other as a shepherd separates the sheep from the goats, and he will place the sheep at his right hand , 'Come, O blest of my father, inherit the kingdom prepared for you, from the foundation of the world; for I was hungry and you gave me food, I was thirsty and you gave me drink, I was a stranger and you welcomed me, I was naked and you clothed me, I was sick and you visited me, I was in prison and you came to me. Then the righteous will answer him. "Lord, when did we see thee hungry and feed thee or thirsty and give you drink? And welcome thee, or naked and clothe thee? And when did we see thee sick or in prison and visit thee? And the King will answer them, 'Truly , I say to you, as you did it to one of the least of these my brethren, you did it to me,' Then he will say to those at his left hand, 'Depart from me you cursed, into the eternal fire prepared for the devil and his angels, for I was hungry and you gave me no food, I was thirsty and you gave me no drink, I was a stranger and you did not welcome me, naked and you did not clothe me, sick and in prison and you did not visit me. Then they also will answer 'Lord when did we see thee hungry, or thirsty, or a stranger or naked or sick or in prison, and did not minister to them? Then he will answer them, "Truly I say to you as you did it not to one of the least of these, you did it not to me' And they will go away into eternal punishment, but the righteous into eternal life." (New Revised Standard Version)]

While this is an excellent example of the social gospel we also note it is an example and summation of apocalyptic literature pertaining to the doctrine of the last times and final judgment common to that day and time (Eschatology).

The letter of James is little utilized today by preachers. James asks: "What does it profit, my brethren, if a man says he has faith and has not works? Can his faith save him? Faith by itself, if it has no works, is dead" (Jas 2: 14–26).

A minister, Washington Gladden, was pastor of the First Congregational Church of Columbus, Ohio, for thirty-two years. His influence during the second half of the nineteenth century was vast among advocates of the social gospel. Likewise, Horace Bushnell was noted as not only a leading theologian regarding the doctrine of the atonement, but also as a pioneer of the importance of the social gospel. In *The Vicarious Sacrifice* (1866) and *Forgiveness and Law* (1874) he stressed the moral theory of the atonement, which liberalism embraced. At his death on Feb 17, 1876, his views were still considered heretical by most contemporaries, but within a few decades his works became regarded as the basic literature for Christ-centered liberalism. Though later liberals altered his ideas, he may rightly be called the father of the liberal movement, which has been so important in Protestant theology in the past century. [1]

Have you ever heard of settlement houses? Of course you have. These were a direct offshoot of the social gospel movement.

Nothing I have said so far is new or original. It is all intended to illustrate that what many people today decry as socialistic is rooted in New Testament theology.

Perhaps the next time someone calls me a socialist I should say "Yes, thank you. I am a socialist. I stand with Jesus of Nazareth."

---

1. Bushnell, *Nature and the Supernatural*, 1858.

Chapter Four

Genesis

Atonement Theology As Godfoolery

WERE IT NOT FOR Eve we would not have need for Jesus. After all, it was Eve who first disobeyed God and ate of the tree of the knowledge of good and evil and it was Eve who shared with Adam the same fruit (Gen 3:8–22).

In the first four chapters of Genesis we have enough "raw" material to create the several theories (really hypotheses) of the atonement as rooted both in the gospels and in the writings of St. Paul.

These theories of atonement form the basis for the necessity of belief in Jesus, later dubbed "The Christ". I intend to demonstrate to the reader that these theories of atonement are entirely the work of biblical scholars and theologians and have little, if anything, to do with the man Jesus. 1 Corinthians 15:21, "For as by a man came death, by a man has come also the resurrection of the dead." Only in later centuries did the church fathers and bishops codify the doctrines that we label today as atonement theories. This is godfoolery.[1]

How was the link established that proclaimed Jesus' death on the cross and subsequent alleged resurrection from the dead a type

---

1. Ehrman, *Lost Christianities*.

of atonement or "paid for" act which frees all humankind from the punishment due for Eve and Adam's disobedience?

The Garden of Eden was in past time—so far past that it is known as pre-history. (For chronologists and biblical scholars historical time begins with Abraham, circa 1900 BC.)[2]

The account of the creation including the linguistic exegesis into JEDP documents (the Documentary Hypothesis) is, for scholars and theologians writing about Adam and Eve and the fruit of the tree, an event of pre-history. Consider: we today have difficulty describing the relatively recent events leading to the rise of Adolf Hitler and Nazism or even to the events preceding the January 6, 2021 insurrection upon the Capitol building in Washington D.C.

The several theories of atonement are still used frequently by Thumpers (popular fundamentalist and evangelical preachers in America especially, of the nineteenth, twentieth, and twenty-first centuries who pound the Bible even as they exhort from it) are just that: theories or hypotheses attempting to explain how Jesus of Nazareth defeated the devil (Christus Victor theory) or how God was now satisfied (Anselm and satisfaction theory) that Jesus' death had atoned for the sins of Eve and Adam or that the punishment due each of us for our disobedience has been paid for by Jesus' sacrifice on the cross (penal substitution). As of this writing there seems to be little use of the moral or exemplar theories.[3] This is part of our current problem. *Today we seem much more concerned to establish theological correctness of a pre-historic event than we are concerned to hold humankind responsible for our own foolishness and poor stewardship in the preservation of the natural order.*

We must ask: Why is it important that modern believers endorse a theology that purports to ensure them that Jesus of Nazareth has allowed himself to be slain so that our sins are forever forgiven and that salvation from death is the reward of the faithful believer? Only by emphasizing sin can today's fundamentalists and evangelicals sell their product of individual salvation.

2. Gehman, *New Westminster Dictionary of the Bible*, 8. See: Gen 12:1.
3. Grinstead, *Short History of the Doctrine of the Atonement*, 11–31.

Really? An alleged event from pre-history combined with purported interpretations from modern times serves to assure humankind believers of their salvation! Church fathers and bishops codify the doctrines that we label today as atonement theories. This is godfoolery.

When will we outgrow the lore and sexist (and racist) tale of Genesis? Not until we rise up and demand that our pastors, preachers, and theologians concentrate on an ethic of self-responsibility. In short, why do we as a nation demand social and personal justice but ignore our own individual responsibility in bringing about social justice that knows no limits or excuses but that impacts all races, colors, income levels, and creeds without limits or lame political games and power maneuvers?

Brief sketches of several prominent theories.

- The Christus Victor theory claims that God, through his son, Jesus, fought with the devil and the son won.[4]
- The ransom theory claims that the devil requires an offering from god as the price that must be paid for the sin of all humanity. This theory is also called the bargain theory because god and the devil are negotiating the price to be paid.
- Anselm (Bishop of Canterbury) is associated with the satisfaction theory. The satisfaction theory directs its logic toward the internal consistency of God's justice. *Dakia* (Greek: justice) is expected of God and therefore by God. In order to achieve justice a price must be paid to the devil in order to satisfy (pay off) the unpaid debt.
- The penal substitution theory. According to this theory all mankind deserves death because all mankind was involved in the sin of Eve and Adam. Jesus' death upon the cross and the ensuing resurrection was held by the devil to be sufficient payment of the debt owed by all humanity, hence Jesus substituted his own life in order that believers should be free of all debt. This theory forms the heart of Martin Luther's famous

---

4. Grinstead, *Short History of the Doctrine of the Atonement*, 11–31.

hymn, *A Mighty Fortress Is Our God.* Also, John Calvin was a key Protestant Reformer who believed strongly in penal substitution.

One of the most ancient theories is known as the moral influence or exemplar theory. Persons such as Friedrich Schleiermacher and in more recent times, Horace Bushnell, represent the most famous personages who have broken with the aforementioned theories of atonement.

Sometimes people misinterpret the exemplar theory to mean that we humans should attempt to be *like* Jesus. This movement is often characterized as people wanting to do what Jesus would do in a similar situation. There are few "similar situations." While this sometimes may be helpful in terms of daily decision making it falls short in terms of governmental standards and political reality.

The idea of exemplar is rooted in the life and death and teachings of Jesus. The gospel of Matthew 5, 6, and 7 is one of the classic synopses of Jesus' teaching. Also, the letter of James. Further, Matthew 25: 31–46 reflects a viable standard of behavior. "When were we thirsty, or without food, clothing, and shelter? Inasmuch as you did not do it to one of the least of these, you did it not to me." (Even as I pen these words in 2021 there remain over five hundred children at the U.S. border near the Rio Grande, many with no beds on which to sleep.) Exemplar indeed! Exemplar theory is not theory at all. It is, however, a standard of ethics and moral behavior to which all men and women and children can relate. After all, it holds them to a standard of personal responsibility.

Many American Christians and Jews often claim the golden rule (the rule of empathy and reciprocity) as their gold standard of personal behavior. Never mind that the golden rule was not first encoded by so-called Christians . It was not considered authentic Jesus material, and it certainly did not originate with him. Quite possibly it was inserted into Jesus' teachings by New Testament redactors, who edited the ancient aphorism. It appears as part of the Sermon on the Mount and the Sermon on the Plain. (Luke 6:31, and it can be found in negative form in Tobit 4:15). What you hate, don't do to someone else.⁵ It appears in one form or another in ancient texts including Hindu texts, Buddhism, Taoism, and Zorastrianism. It was an important facet of the teachings of Confucius and Laozi in ancient China, as well as in India, Egypt and Greece."

Off the Hook Theologies

Atonement preaching is intended to control the listener/believer. When we consider the broad sweep of evangelical/fundamentalist members and believers who subscribe to Christus victor, ransom, satisfaction, and penal substitution we must conclude that their lives are somewhat controlled and governed by their belief that they have already been forgiven and accepted (saved) as blameless in the eyes of god. This means that in their thinking almost anything goes (carte blanche).⁶

It is of paramount importance to note that none of the theories (Christus Victor, satisfaction, ransom, penal substitution) demand or require any action or sacrifice of the individual. The aforementioned atonement theories have the effect of giving humans a clear pass for doing with their lives whatever they darn well please.

Of even greater importance, the only theory of atonement that calls for a life-affirming viral human response is the *exemplar* theory which charges humankind with obligation to incorporate the teachings and ethics of Jesus in everyday reality.

This second advantage of exemplar thinking is the fact that exemplar embraces life itself and the freedom of individuals to create meaning and purpose for themselves and their own families. As a matter of fact, the theories of Christus victor, satisfaction,

---

5. For further amplification of the origins of the golden rule, see Greg Epstein, *Good Without God*, 113.

6. I have heard from several political conservatives that they would endorse Donald J. Trump regardless of his sexual escapades. As my Roman Catholic friend said to me, "John, God's grace can cover an awful lot of sin." Carte blanche indeed.

ransom, and penal substitution can, and often are, seen as a "pass" for doing whatever one pleases.

After I left the ministry of the Presbyterian Church I plied my second career as a professor of Family Development and Family Therapy. My various encounters, both in the counseling room and the classroom (many of my students were seminary students) led me to the conclusion that many of my students saw Genesis as a joke. Authored by God itself and allegedly written down by Moses, it puts words, thoughts, and situations into a theater-like skit that makes God look foolish as he (it) attempts to account for the creation of the earth.

Genesis is nothing except lore.[7] Only in later centuries did the church fathers and bishops codify the doctrines that we label today as lore. Only in later centuries did the church, through its councils and holy synods, seek to translate doctrine into holy offices.

---

7. Crosby, *Faithlore*.

Chapter Five

O Death, Where is Thy Victory?

"Water, water everywhere, and not a drop to drink."[1] *The Rime of the Ancient Mariner* by Samuel Taylor Coleridge has it right. When people thirst for life itself there is no water to be had. At least not in the state of Georgia. At least not in March, 2021 when the Georgian governor signed a bill making it unlawful to give water to anyone standing in line to vote. No, no, no. To give water would be life-sustaining and to be life-sustaining would be contrary to the ambitions and ethics of the political party that will do anything to regain lost power.

Perhaps it is not water at all, but a way to avenge Sherman's march to the sea in 1865. Perhaps this political trick is a way to avenge Appomattox itself when a way of life was supposedly erased from the North American continent.

Maybe Margaret Mitchell was *wrong* about a civilization "*Gone With the Wind?*" Perhaps the fiasco in Georgia was really a demand that slavery be resurrected and the old order restored. Perhaps the original constitution of the United States was on the right track when a person of color was counted as being only *three fifths* of a person rather than a whole person? In reality, maybe the three/fifths was a high water mark. In truth, we seem to be going backward.

---

1 Coleridge, *Rime of the Ancient Mariner*, 20.

Suddenly I wonder what happened to the bystander who held up a reed with a sponge filled with vinegar for the dying Jesus to taste! (Matt 27:48).

I ask repeatedly, O death where is thy victory? O death where is thy sting? (1 Corinthians 15: 55). The more likely translation is "O Death, where is thy victory? O *Sheol,* where is thy sting?"

In all seriousness. Are we stuck in a Jim Crow mentality?

Chapter Six

You Won't Be Disappointed

I DO NOT KNOW much for sure.

I think I know, with Descartes, that "I think. Therefore I am."

I know that my mind somehow creates my reality. This is to say I know reality, or what I call reality, is comprehended by me, or perceived by me, only through the agency of my mind. Whatever that is. Authorities disagree. But I do know that without my mind there would be no me. I am much influenced by the three British empiricists, Locke, Berkeley, and Hume. Especially Hume, from whom I probably learned my heavy dose of skepticism.

But now that I am in my ninth decade I have lately become absolutely convinced that I need have no fear of death. This is because I am certain (if certainty be an option) that I will not be disappointed.

I will not be disappointed about meeting up with my parents, especially my dad, with whom I would like to discuss the meaning of it all and the whys and wherefores of his early preachments to me. He will probably be busy talking with his Dad.

I will not be disappointed about my new lodgings and the surrounding habitat of my new existence or about my new circle of companions and friends, Democrats and Republicans, believers and atheists, agnostics and skeptics.

I will not be disappointed.

Which prompts me to ask,

You Won't Be Disappointed

What about you?
Are you at peace? With yourself I mean.
Let me share something with you. Just one thing. Just to set your mind at ease.
You will not be disappointed. No you won't.
You will not be disappointed about your parents.
Or your siblings.
Or your children
Or your country.
Or your political party.
Or your lodgings.
Or you companions and friends.
Or former wife or husband.
Or those who didn't like you or bullied you, hurt you, or cheated you.
Or about whether or not there is a heaven or a hell.
No, you will not be disappointed.
How could you be?
To be disappointed demands that you have a *consciousness*.
An awareness.
A clue as to what is going on.
But you will not be disappointed because—
Well, in case you haven't figured it out (I wish to be delicate on this point), you will be quite dead!
This is to say,
You will be quite dead.
Therefore, you are deceased and without consciousness,
or memory,
or recall,
or any other synonym for nothingness, emptiness or non-existence.
So please tell me, how could you ever be disappointed?
YOU WON'T BE DISAPPOINTED
About whether or not there is a heaven or a hell.
No, you will not be disappointed.
How could you be?

Nor will you be overjoyed.

To be disappointed implies that somehow or other you have a consciousness, an awareness.

This is to say you will not be disappointed because—

    You are quite dead.
    You have no clue as to what is gong on.
    You are deceased and without consciousness,
    or memory,
    or recall,
    or any other synonym for nothingness, emptiness or non-existence.

So please tell me, how could you ever be disappointed?

    Or overjoyed?

Or vindicated?

Or accused?

You simply will not be!

You will have simply returned to nature;

You will have become part of the natural order.

In short YOU WILL NOT BE...."

CHAPTER SEVEN

Theodicy

*Making Excuses for God and Explaining
and Defending the God Hypothesis*

I WAS THRILLED IN 1956 when the Presbytery of Mahoning ordained me. I was thrilled even more in 1970 when the Presbytery of Cayuga-Syracuse voted to join me in my petition to be relieved of my ordination vows.

To others, including a few close friends, I must have looked forlorn right after the vote was taken. I walked down the center aisle of that church, heads bowed but still peeking at me. I was not forlorn. I was happy! I was overjoyed inside! I was now free of all holy orders or whatever the call to the ministry of Jesus Christ was currently being called.

Far away in Ohio my parents would be grieving. I'm sure they thought they had lost their oldest son. They were devout Presbyterians of the moralistic variety. They thought they knew a lot about ministers because of their minister friends. Their view was extremely romanticized.

Dad and Mom, please believe me, I did not feel lost! I felt quite the contrary. I felt alive again. I felt free. Free from promises made in 1956 at my ordination about accepting the historic *Westminster Confession of Faith* wherein I gave myself to the ministry of Jesus Christ and to his church, I now felt a terrible burden had been lifted from my shoulders. Chapter eight will outline in specific detail some of the more difficult and poignant situations in which I was involved.

My basic problem within the church was not church administration or in crafting sermons. What I clearly did not like to do was make promises or even suggestions that I could not keep! In short my labors at the sickbed and the deathbed were in vain.

My most severe problem was theodicy. How could a just god allow this to happen? How can a just god allow the many wars recorded in the Old Testament? How could a just and loving god permit the crusades, including the Childrens crusade? Shall we mention the Holocaust? Hitler? Stalin? The twin towers of 9/11? The flood as recorded in Genesis? Or Job? Or the Ukraine? If god is truly omnipotent and all powerful and all knowing then what excuse or reason is there for not only man-made evil but the evils of nature itself? Earthquakes, wind, and fire? Hurricanes, tornadoes, floods, ptsunamies?

Theodicy means literally, "God's justice." (*Theos* (Greek: god) joined with *dic'y* or *dikare'* (justice).

Without such authorities as confessions and creeds where do we begin? If we start at the beginning we must turn to physics and astrophysics. We must focus on novas and black holes. We must focus on every conceivable interpretation of how the galaxies and other systems spun off into orbit. Perhaps the deists among us would be satisfied to retreat to the simplistic watchmaker view of god wherein god creates the watch, winds it up, and then goes off and occupies his mind with some other challenge, allowing the watch to run by itself and do its own thing.

If we retreat to the watchmaker line of reasoning we will have no problem with theodicy simply because the watchmaker god is transcendent but not immanent. Hence there does not need be any expectation of "justness" and mercy and empathy within the created order.

We must rest assured that such things as suffering and pain and massive destruction are not part of the formation of the universe or multiverse.

THEODICY

Everything boils down to the question of immanence and the interpersonal involvement of the creative life force in the lives and affairs of beings such as ourselves. I solved the problem of theodicy for myself by rejecting the monotheistic definitions of god common to religions such as Islam, Judaism, and Christianity. I rejected, and still reject, all "revealed" religion. The nonbeliever can have no problem with theodicy simply because the nonbeliever denies the existence of a god figure. By definition, only the believer can have a problem with theodicy because only if a person chooses to believe in god is there a problem of evil and suffering.

Whatever is "revealed" had to be written down by someone. Whoever wrote it down was the real culprit, be they monks and scholars, be they modern day professors and priests or ancient scribes and apologists.

No longer do I need to defend the actions or non-actions of some man-made deity whom I am not supposed to question or challenge as Job did. One of the clearest examples of editorial redaction to the Old Testament is in Job 38-42. Even Job's three well-meaning friends serve to show how little support poor Job received (Eliphaz, Bildad, and Zophar, Job 4, 7, and 11). Essentially they told Job he was full of it. With friends like these, who needs enemies? Even Job's wife turned on Job. In Job 2:9 She says to Job, "Do you still hold fast your integrity? Curse God and die." Wow! What wonderful support from one's wife!

The redactors could not let Job win his debate with god because Job was winning! So a complete new ending was added to Job which would forever serve to prove that Job was irreverent and way off the track of true (blind) faith. God says, "Where were you when I laid the foundation of the earth?"(38:4). Then Job recants and caves in. Job's wealth is apparently quadrupled. God wins!

Chapter Eight

Four Strikes And You're Out

Here follows what I regret *not saying* to my parents.

I regret not taking them with me as I made numerous hospital visits.

And cemetery appearances.

And telling them about numerous counseling hours.

I regret not sharing more with them.

I would say to them that I found myself woefully unprepared to enter into the inner lives and fears and problems of young people and older people.

Oh yes, I had been well-trained in terms of New Testament theology, Old Testament theology, Greek, Hebrew, church history and the history of Christianity.

Then I would tell them about four events that shaped the rest of my life.

Strike I. Sally

Sally had come to me for counseling. Her distress was obvious in that she appeared agitated and extremely ill at ease. I met with Sally on two occasions and finally recommended she see a psychiatrist. Sometime after helping her make these arrangements she phoned me to tell me she was feeling better.

About a week after the phone call she came to my church office and said, "Guess what? He (the doctor) dismissed me."

Here was my first mistake. If nothing else, I should have phoned the doctor to confirm the dismissal.

Three days later about 6:00 a.m. I received a phone call from Sally's husband. Sally was dead. An overdose of prescribed medications.

In a matter of hours the grieving husband and I agreed that we would not tell the two children, age about six and nine, that Sally had taken her own life. This was a stupid decision on my part. As of this writing I still regret this decision.

Strike II. David

David as a lively seven-year-old. Second born. From the time of his birth heart surgery had been planned. I do not recall the prognosis but the surgery was considered "normal" and routine. It would be when David was aged seven, at a New York City hospital. I can't remember if it was Presbyterian or Columbia.

I visited with the family and David before they departed Syracuse. In late afternoon on the day of surgery I received a phone call informing me that all had gone well. Then, at 3:00 a.m. my phone rang. I knew it was bad news. David was dead. Someone, I was told, inserted a by-pass tube into the wrong vein or artery in David's groin. The result was death.

When the family arrived back in Syracuse I walked to their nearby home. It was a cold, snowy evening. I recall being with the family and I recall the father saying he wished he could be with Davy in heaven. When the father persisted I (regretfully) mentioned that David's passing was somehow connected to the *will of God*.

As I walked home I could hear the crunch of the hardened snow beneath my feet. Then I recalled what I had said about the will of god. Suddenly, I felt sick. So sick I stopped dead in my tracks and vomited right there in the snow. I have never believed

David's death was the will of god and to this day I bitterly regret having said those words.

Strike III. Charles

Charles was a very lively and a very normal teenager. During the famous blizzard of 1966 Charles wanted to go out in the blizzard and cut through the woods to his girlfriend's home. His father stood at the door and forbade him. Charles countered that it was o.k. because his father had taught him how to wear and use special snow shoes. (the kind hat look like tennis rackets). Into the blizzard went sixteen-year-old Charley—into oblivion.

I recall going on two searches for Charley in the first several days after the blizzard. I was hoping I would not be the one to find him. Thankfully, it was his father who found Charles, sitting peacefully up against a small tree at the end of the hedgerow. I was later criticized by a member of the church for being on the search. I guess I should have been at home praying, as was suggested by a loyal church member.

Strike IV. Ken

Ken was a member of the church and he and I bonded together as we searched though a dark and thick woods, about five miles from the village center. We were always to search in "twos". We were searching for young Ralph, who suffered from a severe mental condition known as schizophrenia. It was believed that young Ralphie, as he was known, had simply responded to a voice within, calling him into the wild.

Good news! Ralphie was soon discovered unharmed and well.

But, several weeks later, still in winter's icy grip, my buddy Ken was hit head-on by another vehicle driving the wrong way on a divided highway in a snow storm as Ken drove home from Syracuse.

Four Strikes And You're Out

I recall how angry I was as I officiated at Ken's funeral. The words came hard even though I had carefully written them out. I cried. Even from the pulpit.

What I have written in the paragraphs above are symbolic of the tragic events that befall almost any clergyman. Looking back, if the above four tragic events had been spaced a bit further apart than eighteen months I might have survived, but no. I did not survive. The events were what they were!

At a graveside service between the above events III and IV I pronounced the final benediction. The deceased was a gentleman in his 70s. I spoke forth:

> Cherishing memories that are forever sacred, sustained by a faith stronger than death, We commit the body of our loved one now departed: tenderly, reverently, and lovingly, in the sure and certain hope of eternal life, through our Lord Jesus Christ. Amen.

I turned away from the casket and walked up the earthen rise when I heard an inner voice loud and clear: The voice was *my* voice and it rang clear and sharp. "Expletive! Expletive! I don't believe a word of it!" To this day I believe that the voice was one part of my brain speaking to another part of my brain. I walked on a few steps. "I then decided in the matter of a few seconds that I was getting out!" I thought: "I don't believe a word of it and I simply am not going to do this any more. No more god business." I was bitter!

Dear reader: "Say what you will! Think what you will. For me it was Game Over."

I went home and shared with Marjorie what I had experienced. She listened as she always did. That night I phoned my father-in-law and told him about my decision. (I had worked for Marj's dad when I was a student at Princeton Seminary). I cried. Really cried. I have not cried since, except at Marjs' death. My decision was irrevocable. I would resign my position as minister. Marj would return to her profession of nursing. Later she would do a masters degree and become a nurse-midwife. For now, I would enroll in a Ph.D. program at Syracuse. My three wonderful sons would survive. I could teach and/or become part of a marriage/

family therapy program. I was still young. Born in 1931 and leaving the ministry in 1967. Actually, the Presbyterian process of leaving would extend to 1970.

I put myself into psychotherapy for a period of one year. I wanted to discover what led me into the ministry and what rewards (ego rewards) had kept me going for these many years. My beloved father was leery of this decision. He warned me against becoming too dependent on the therapist. He also made it clear that he and Mom would not or could not support me financially. This came to me as no surprise. In my planning I never considered that my folks would help me. They were both crushed and extremely disappointed. Marjorie's folks were quite supportive of me.

My Mom, especially, seemed to be heartbroken. At one point, when I explained to them that I was not just resigning my job in the local Presbyterian church, but that I was *demitting* the ministry (Presbyterian term for de-frocking oneself), my mother, never given to screaming or loud protestations, blurted out: "Oh John, can't you wait until we're dead?" Her voice and demeanor still resonate in my mind today. I dare say, things were never the same again although Mom and Dad seemed to enjoy my role in marriage and family studies at Indiana University and (Mom only) at the University of Kentucky. Dad had passed.

Yes, I regret that I did not take the lead with my parents. I wish I could do it over. But, of course, I can't.

CHAPTER NINE

Tribalism and White Supremacy

WE ALL LEARNED THAT the American Civil War ended at Appomattox Court House on Friday, April 9, 1865. We now know that some things related to the war have never been resolved. Yes, officers were permitted to keep their horses. Guns (mostly rifles) were surrendered. General Joe Johnstons' army in North Carolina had not yet surrendered but would do so within a week. Abraham Lincoln would be assassinated on Friday, April 14, 1865.

The new President would be Vice President Andrew Johnson.

Lincoln's Revised Emancipation Proclamation had been released on January 1, 1863, four months following the historic battle of Antietam. All people of color residing in any state or portion thereof no longer in rebellion against the Union were now theoretically free.

The thirteenth amendment (1865) to the Constitution states: "Neither slavery nor involuntary servitude except as punishment for having been convicted of a crime, is allowed in the United States or in any of its territories or possessions."

But hold on! Was the war really over? No! Not in the hearts and minds of white men. It rages today under the guise of lip service to the slogan "All Lives Matter" (a white supremacy phrase that conveniently dismisses the idea that our nation has historically ignored the rights and welfare of its Black and Brown citizens). The purpose of this chapter is to examine how completely and how powerfully racism has become entrenched in the white

American (especially) male psyche. This racism is in reality nothing but white supremacy and white nationalism.

Is it over yet? Not by a long shot. The ending of slavery is one thing. Granting people of color the right to vote in all civil elections without hindrance of any kind is something else, a right being quickly eroded in some of our southern states. So the key questions become, where and when did white supremacy begin? And why did we ever tolerate it? In short, why do we have a history of hatred and violence toward people of color? And why does it continue?

I am writing this chapter from the point of view of radical constructivism, a belief that so-called absolute objective reality does exist but that this reality can be assessed only as the result of the interactive processing of neurons, synapses, and neurotransmitters within the human brain. This does not mean there is no ultimate reality. It means that our only approach to that reality is through our brain, that is, access to any kind of reality is possible only through the intermediate agency of the human brain. It is in this sense that we create or invent our reality.[1] Of course this translates into the fact that each of us has our own sense of reality and that mine may be drastically different than yours It is not an exaggeration to say that there is a democratic reality and a republican reality and further, a conservative Republican party of Lincoln reality and another Republican party of Trumpian reality, a party of racism and white supremacy.[2]

Stamped From The Beginning, a book by Ibram X. Kendi[3] is the most comprehensive book I have found on the subject of racism and white supremacy. Kendi treats the subject from the perspective of two approaches: Antiracism in the form of segregation, and antiracism in the form of assimilation. "For nearly six centuries antiracists ideas have been pitted against two kinds of racist ideas: segregationist and assimilationist. The history of racial ideas that follows is the history of these distinct voices—segregationists,

---

1. Crosby, *Faithlore*, Chapter 4. And *Flipside of Godspeak*, Chapter 1 and 2.

2. Von Glasersfeld, *Radical Constructivism*. Also, Watzlawick, *Invented Reality*.

3. Kendi, *Stamped From the Beginning*.

Tribalism and White Supremacy

assimilationist and how they each have rationalized racial disparities, arguing why Whites have remained on the living and winning end, while Blacks have remained on the losing and dying end."[4]

Further, Kendi builds his argument upon the historical records of five "tour guides." These tour guides serve as nails or hooks upon which he builds his subsequent points of affirmation. These five "tour guides," beginning with Cotton Mather and extending through Thomas Jefferson, William Lloyd Garrison, W.E.B. DuBois, and Angela Davis are each integral to the themes stated above, i.e. antiracism in the form of segregation, and assimilation. Sidebar I is a personal statement by Kendi.

> I was taught the popular folktale of racism: that ignorant and hateful people had produced racist ideas, and that these racist people had instituted racist policies. But when I learned the motives behind the production of many of America's most influentially racist ideas, it became quite obvious that this folktale, though sensible, was not based on a firm footing of historical evidence. Ignorance->racist ideas->discrimination: this causal relationship is largely ahistorical. It has actually been the inverse relationship—racial discrimination led to racist ideas which led to ignorance and hate. Racial discrimination -> racist ideas ->which led to ignorance/hate: this is the causal relationship driving America's history of race relations.
>
> Their own racist ideas usually did not dictate the decisions of the most powerful Americans when they instituted, defended, and tolerated discriminatory policies that affected millions of Black lives over the course of American history. Racially discriminatory policies have usually sprung from economic, political, and cultural self-interests that are constantly changing. [1]
>
> 1. Kendi, *Stamped From the Beginning*, 8–9.

Kendi goes on to claim that politicians, capitalists, theologians, artists, scholars, and journalists have embraced and defended discriminatory policies out of professional self interest—not racist ideas.[5] And thus, we were taught that our own interests, be

---

4. Kendi, *Stamped From the Beginning*, 2.
5. Kendi, *Stamped From the Beginning*, 10.

they professional or not, were not racist but simply for our own good.

However, we must ask, where is personal conscience in all of this? Where is the cultural and societal sense of honor and morality? Is racism excused by simply writing it off as being in our (white people's) best interest? I think there is more to it than that.

1. There is the white person's thirst for *power* (control, dominance).

2. There is the white person's *Oxi authentikos* (Greek for "no attractiveness" about the brown/black race or "unattractiveness" as determined by white standards).

3. And there is *ignorance* in the extreme, giving rise to fear. The greater our ignorance and the greater our misinformation the greater is the likelihood of fear for our own safety and fear of unscrupulous authority.

4. However, and most importantly, the underlying foundation for each of the above factors of causation is tribalism. Tribalism is the joining together of people of like-minded persuasion who act always in the best interests of the tribe without question of morality, (right or wrong), legality, or loyalty to other powers, principalities, and kinship groups.

Figure 1 illustrates the role and position of tribalism as it undergirds the rise of *Oxi authentikos*, ignorance/fear and power/control.

An illustration of the role and position of tribalism as it undergirds the rise of *oxi authentikos*, ignorance/fear, and power/control.

A tracing of the history of the slave trade shows a beginning in the eastern African nations south and west of the Sahara. From the beginning it was a matter of force, power, and capture and then ship by sea to receptive ports and nations. The history of the slave traders and the slave-trading vessels is not a "comfortable read." Countries such as Ethiopia, Arabia, Egypt, the Netherlands, Portugal, Spain, and Italy, in addition to Great Britain were involved.[6]

The foundation of almost everything that follows is, in my analysis, best described as tribalism. I rely heavily on George Packer's article in the *New Yorker* as being one of the most penetrating and comprehensive on tribalism.[7] I also draw on Sebastian

---

6. Kandi, *Stamped From the Beginning*, 1–11, 15–65.
7. Packer, "New Report Offers Insights into Tribalism in the Age of Trump."

Younger's *Tribe*,[8] Ron Newby's *Tribalism*.[9] and Isabel Wilkerson's *Caste*.[10]

My own early acquaintance with tribe was as a devoted fan of the Cleveland Indians baseball team. The connection with American Indians was, of course, not much on my young mind. Later, in college, I became a part of a tribe that helped me grow up and mature. My tribe was a non-secret fraternity dedicated to justice and responsible manhood.[11]

Athletics and the growth of both college and professional sports are illustrative of tribal thinking and tribal behavior. For millions of people tribal identity is a diversion from the reality of everyday work and arduous labor. Whether you are a Yankee fan or a partner in the Green Bay football organization the idea of tribe gives rise to strong ties of identity and belonging. Soccer in England and the continent, especially, brings one's sense of self to the point of pride and self-power. It is not too far out to say that sports teams, from little leagues to Super Bowls to World Series, may serve as a diversion from many of life's hardships and challenges. So, the idea or concept of a tribe may be a good thing, but not if it results in a prejudicial tribalism that too often becomes harmful and hateful.

A *destructive* tribe embraces an entirely negative value system, one that can quickly transform its constituents into tribes of violence and bitter rivalry. Sports tribes may morph into destructive and irrational repositories of hatred and bitterness, bringing opponents to the brink of physical combat and riot when things get out of hand. On the other hand constructive and participatory diversions such as chess, bridge playing, and grass/field sports

---

8. Younger, *Tribe*.
9. Newby, *Tribalism*.
10. Wilkerson, *Caste*.
11. *Delta Upsilon*. We had our share of problems but my experience as chapter president at Denison remains one of those experiences that contribute to maturity and respect for organizational authority and differing viewpoints. I would classify it as a constructive tribe.

such as shuffle board, crochet, lawn tennis, and pickle ball may perform a healthy and wholesome social function.

President Andrew Jackson had a negative and harmful American view of tribalism, which to this day brings terrible memories of tales about the "trail of tears" and how President Jackson acted ruthlessly and without compassion when he mandated the removal of many southeastern native Indian tribes to regions west of the Mississippi River.

The twelve tribes of Israel in contrast to Jackson's merciless treatment of the native Indian tribes gave us quite opposite perspectives on tribalism.

The Genesis accounts of the Hebrew enslavement in Egypt give us an account of government and the internal organization of the Hebraic tribes.

> The forefathers of the people of Israel had descended into Egypt as a family of 12 households, and had settled together in Goshen.... They did not assimilate with the master race, (The Egyptians) but remained a distinct people and preserved the twelve great family divisions. By the end of the 430 years, the families of the 12 sons had become 12 tribes , and the son's sons, and in a few instances the sons' remoter descendants, had grown into large family, at the time of the exodus connections. Accordingly, at the time of the exodus there was a people, Israel, divided into 12 tribes, and each tribe was subdivided into families or connections, which derived their names for the most part from the grandsons of Jacob...
>
> Authority of various kinds was vested in leaders by birth, heads of the tribes or family connections, elders, who were probably heads of tribes or families; and aged, apparently also in priests. ...The people of Israel, grouped also in tribes, families, and fathers' houses, officered and accustomed to obedience, were not an unwieldy horde, but a multitude with the organization of an army.[1]

1. Gehman, *New Westminster Dictionary of the Bible*, 251.

The distinction between tribe and tribalism is best described as a distinction of order and organized management and civil cooperation as with the tribes of Israel compared to ordinary "isms" that often point to raw power, abuse of human rights, and civil administration such as communism and all kinds of fascism .

Sebastian Younger points out that *belonging* is central to tribal reality. If we did not belong to the mother who bore us we would not have survived. Yes, there have been nannies and wet nurses but in ordinary terms, our very survival depends first of all upon a very particular form of tribe, the nuclear family, and later, the extended family.

I proceed with the assumption that many tribes are positive creations of social living. These are constructive examples of tribes. These may include the Quakers, the Mennonites, the Amish, the Owenites, the Rappites, the Pilgrims, the Mormons, the Islamic and Hebraic religions, and the countless varieties of Protestant and Roman Catholic Christians. There are also destructive examples of tribes and tribalism. Examples include negative instances of forces and situations that are harmful to humanity, even a threat to our survival on planet earth. History bears witness to the reality of tribes that are life-affirming as well as tribes that are life destructive. Two of the very worst of all such tribes in recent memory are those of Adolf Hitler and of Donald J. Trump.

People ask me: What about Trump and Trumpism? My reply is simple. Trump has created a cult about himself that brooks no dissent from his authoritarian quest for power. This, in itself, creates the tribal myth of Trumpism sustained by the tribal threat (mostly to senators and representatives) of tribal ostracism of apostates and unbelievers. The Big Lie is, of course, a lie. Nevertheless the lie is power laden because senators, representatives, and all kinds of political appointees want desperately to be a part of Trump's demented reality, i.e. his tribe, wherein there is no tolerance for dissent. Truth be damned. Truth is "created reality."

The United States is no longer a two party system wherein differing rationalities vie for public endorsement at the polls. America has a progressive tribe that is committed to positive human values including a fair and equitable distribution of wealth and personal enrichment, e.g. the feminist tribe committed to gender equality and equity. The progressive tribe affirms life and the radical financial tribe affirms a right to have an ever expanding level of income.

Each tribe is founded upon a belief system. The progressive tribe affirms life and the demented tribe affirms wealth in spite of so-called religious values. Any fair examination of values (axiology) places these two tribes in stark opposition to each other. The Trumpian tribe solution to power is to prevent and/or discourage the progressive tribes from voting. In other words, the strategic and tactical goal of the Trumpian tribes is to disenfranchise the progressive tribes. This is the heart-bed of racism and white supremacy.

In order for the Trump tribe to gain and hold power it must demonstrate its ability to control the economy and the thinking of the masses who would share his enthronement. In order to do this Trump must hold to his belief in white supremacy and white nationalism. It is at this point that tribal endorsement of anti-inellectualism plus widespread ignorance and fear, irrespective of evidence to the contrary, combine in the name of Trumpism to dominate and control the American mind.

There is one other building block arising out of the foundation of Trumpian tribalism. (See Figure 1) *Oxi authentikos* is a Greek double word, meaning, literally, "unattractive." (*Oxi*, "no" and *authentikos*, "attractiveness"). With a foundation of tribal loyalty giving rise to power, ignorance, and fear, it is a small and easy step to embrace the superiority of the white race. This is especially true if the black and brown races, including races of American Indian, Latin, and Spanish descent as well as religions of Islamic belief, are believed to be unattractive (i.e. *Oxi authentikos*)[12] by white people.

---

12. Several words may be used for my purpose. Uncomely or unseemly, *aschemon* (1 Cor 12:23) *asxhemon* (Koine Greek).

Godfoolery

George Packer begins his penetrating analysis of tribalism:

> American politics today requires a word as primal as 'tribe' to get at the blind allegiances and huge passions of partisan affiliation. Tribes demand loyalty, and in return they confer the security of belonging. They're badges of identity, not of thought. In a way they make thinking unnecessary, because they do it for you, and may punish you if you try and do it for yourself. To get along without a tribe makes you a fool. To give an inch to the other tribe makes you a sucker.[1]

And so today Americans are divided by thoughtless allegiance to propositions that lead to destruction. The tribes today have no respect for each other, even to the point of storming the Capitol building in Washington, D.C, in order to nullify the certification of an election. The tribal leader, Trump, set himself up as a champion of all those who endorse him.[2] This again reflects the ignorance and blind acceptance of all Trumpian beliefs and the blindness of all Trumpian tribalism.

As Ron Newby states, "One would think politics is simply about governing, but fundamentally it has to do with the distribution of wealth of the nation. Any analysis of governances would discover a discernable amount of deception, graft, and hanky-panky. Compared to other forms of governing, democracy, even with consideration of all its foibles, remains very successful in the metrics of public acceptance and outcome. Could there be a more fair and equitable form of governance? Everyone has an opinion based upon objectively collected evidence, or it may be based on religious or political tenants not subject to inspection or denial. What seems clear is, we are politically tribal and changing political tribes is a rare event. The future is not rosy."[3]

---

1. Packer, "New Report Offers Insights Into Tribalism In The Age Of Trump."
2. I wish I had taken courses and participated in debate while I was in high school and college. The opportunity was there but I was too immature to take advantage. It is in this sense that we lack true debate with Donald Trump. Trump has no concept of true debate and rational intellectual intercourse. (Nor did Hitler or Stalin)
3. Newby, Tribalism, 186.

Tribalism and White Supremacy

In these paragraphs I have set out to address the question of white supremacy. I conclude by stating that Trumpian tribalism preys on the alleged non-attractiveness of the non-white population. This is a stark and unwelcome conclusion. Only under certain conditions can so-called biblical evidence be accepted . The Ham story is simply "lore" and lacks credible evidence.[13] Cultural beliefs regarding solar temperatures in western and central Africa are useless and intellectually disrespected explanations.

Modern North American tribalism seizes on the period of reconstruction after Lincoln's death as being the most damning decade in the collective growth of North American belief in white supremacy and superiority. In short, belief in white supremacy is a belief in the inferiority and alleged *oxi authentikos* of the black race, a *despicable* belief giving power and credence to destructive tribalism.

---

13. Gehman, *New Westminster Dictionary of the Bible*, 359. See Genesis 5:32, 6:10, and 9:21. At the time of the deluge he (Ham) was married but apparently had no children (Gen 7:7, 1 Peter 3:20) On the occasion of his father's drunkenness he behaved undutifully (viewed his father's nakedness) and in curred a curse to descend upon Canaan. The list of peoples of south Arabia, Ethiopia, Egypt, and Canaan includes both his descendants and those acquired by conquest and political annexation.

Chapter Ten

Bible Stories Not Learned in Sunday School

Onan Suffered the Death Penalty *for* Coitus Interruptus

ONANS' BROTHER ER, JUDAH'S first-born son, had died. Er's wife was now widowed. Judah then told his second son, Onan, to perform the duty of the Leverite and to be as a husband to his widowed sister-in-law, Tamar.

The *Leverite* was a Jewish-Hebrew practice wherein a younger brother is duty-bound to perform the duties of a husband with a dead brother's widow. (The dead brother was usually an older brother.) Therefore, Onan was charged with the responsibility of impregnating his deceased brother's wife, Tamar (Gen 38:8–10 NRSV).

Onan, to a point, attempted to fulfill this responsibility. He went into her. So we can conclude that Onan was sexually stimulated to the point were he had an erection. Nevertheless, before Onan reached the point of ejaculation, he withdrew his penis from Tamar and allowed his spermatic ejaculate to spurt upon the ground (or the bed, or the forest floor, or the backseat of the Chevy).

This was displeasing in the sight of the Lord. And he (the Lord) slew him (Onan) also. Now both of Judah's sons, are dead.

> It appeared at that time that Judah went down from his brothers and settled in a certain Adalamite whose name was Hirah...Judah took a wife for Er, his first born; But Er, Judah's first born, was wicked in the sight of the Lord, and the Lord put him to death. Then Judah said to Onan "Go into your brother's wife and perform the duty of a brother in law to her, raise up offspring for your brother. But since Onan knew that the offspring would not be his, he spilled his semen on the ground whenever he went into his brother's wife, so that he would not give offspring to his brother. What he did was displeasing in the sight of the Lord, and he (the Lord) put him to death also. ...So Tamara went to live in her father's house. (Actually, her father-in-law's house) (Gen 38: 1–11 NRSV) (The reader can read the rest of the story.)

In the years since, Onan's rebellious act of withdrawal (scientifically labeled as *coitus interruptis)* has been considered an act of disobedience, an act which was an affront to the Lord.

The Roman Catholic Church considered Onan's act of penile withdrawal as being equivalent to masturbation and, as such, has henceforth been considered it to be sinful. Today many Protestant churches and conservative Protestant congregations and ministers, likewise consider *coitus interruptis* as being equivalent to masturbation.

I have chosen to retell this story because there has scarcely been a male child who, in his early years of physical development, has not experienced a wet dream. Completely involuntary, the boy awakes from sleep after spewing forth an amount of semen containing millions of sperm. Typically, if the young boy has not been prepared for this surprising event, he will attempt to hide it from his mother or whomever changes the bed sheets. If he has not been prepared, he may conclude that there is something wrong with his body. Yet, the ejaculation is such that its rapturous feeling and sensation is bound to cause confusion and wonderment.

Or, he may learn from his buddies and other friends.

I was in my final year as an ordained minister in the Presbyterian Church when a lady cornered me after the Sunday service and asked me in a rather earnest manner, would I please meet with her eleven-year-old son Glen and inform him about the facts of life. "You know," she said, "Explain to him all about the birds and the bees."

Actually, I had been asked to do many things as a minister that I really didn't mind doing, but this was a real challenge. I did not know this lady nor was her son a part of our youth group. And I don't think I ever saw them again.

What to tell him? How to explain it? Oh sure, I was the father of three sons. This would be a piece of cake! But no! This turned out to be a great deal more difficult than "just a piece of cake." I wished I had props of some kind. But no, that would be considered bad practice. And all the books were too intellectual and too long. Pictures were considered pornographic.

The appointed time having arrived, Glen walked into my office with an "air" of authority and perhaps of disdain. It was almost as if he were saying, "This is silly. Why do I have to be here?"

I began the conversation: "Your mother didn't tell me much about your coming here. What did she say to you?"

"Nothin really" . . . "except, you know , my father is dead and mother seems to think I need to talk to a man about...."

Glen went into a long pause.

"Well, you might just as well know..... she seems not able to talk about man things and besides, I know all about it."

I replied, "about *it*."

"Yeah, you know, about sex."

"Suppose we start and you simply tell me about what you know."

"Well, I know about sexual intercourse and about how men squirt their sperm into the girl's muff." But what I didn't know was, (pause) "Well, this is embarrassing, I did not know the sperm stuff would come out of me all by itself while I was sleeping."

From that point on Glen went on without much encouragement from me.

We parted after about an hour—friends who had sized each other up!

I never heard from nor saw Glen or his mother again.

In conclusion, masturbation is natural and normal.[1] Masturbation is not sinful or wrong or dirty. It is not credited with a fool proof label for preventing pregnancy. However, when a male masterbates privately without the presence of a female it is likely 100 percent effective as a deterrent to pregnancy. I have known male clients who claimed they masturbated before going to a function wherein they knew with some certainty that they could be tempted. I have known male clients who frequently did sex play and mutual masturbation prior to functions that employed women of ill repute in order to reduce the threshold of their own vulnerability to temptation.

Our biblical friend, Onan, gave up his life because he was intelligent and informed about the mission of sperm. He made it clear he did not wish to be a father to a child of Tamar.

Many churches and other religious institutions disdain truth and teach their own doctrine about sperm and sexual intercourse as a means of control over the behavior of their young people. Rigid prohibitions and serious attempts at mind control can result in later years of sexual frustration and interpersonal hangups, even with one's mate.

---

1. The subject is well-covered on the internet.

Chapter Eleven

Bible Stories Not Learned in Sunday School

King David Has His Way with Bathsheba and Then Arranges for Her Husband to Be Killed in Battle.

GET OUT YOUR BIBLE. Almost any version or translation will do. I will use NRSV, the *New Revised Standard Version*.

Go to 2 Samuel. Chapters 11 and 12.

I will make it easy for you. I will tell you a story. As I relate the story I will explain the plot that David carries out and I will quote only the most relevant verses.

It happened, late one afternoon, when David rose from his couch and was walking about on the roof of the king's house, when he saw from the roof a woman bathing. The woman was very beautiful. David sent someone to inquire about the woman. The messenger reported back to David: "This is Bathsheba, the daughter of Eliam, the wife of Uriah the Hittite."

So David sent messengers to get her, and she came to him, and he lay with her. (she was purifying herself after her period.) The woman conceived; and told David, "I am pregnant."

Then David sent word to Joab. "Send me Uriah the Hittite," And Joab sent Uriah to David. When Uriah came to him, David asked Uriah how Joab and the people fared . . . Uriah answered that the soldiers were camping in the fields, sleeping in booths.

However, and this is the kicker, Uriah slept at the entrance of the king's house with all the servants of his lord. He did not go down to his own house as David had suggested.

This news upset David. "When they told David Uriah did not go down to his house, David said to Uriah "You have just come from a journey. Why did you not go down to your house?" Uriah said to David. The ark and Israel and my lord Joab remain in booths[1] and my lord and the servants of my lord are encamping in the open field; shall I then go to my house, to eat and to drink, and to lie with my wife? As you live, and as your soul lives, I will not do such a thing."

In other words, Uriah, faithful soldier that he was, refused to go to his house to eat and drink and lie with his wife, while his troops were sleeping near the battlefield in little booths, hut-like shelters made of tree branches.

But why, we must ask, would King David order Uriah to go home, especially on the eve of battle?

Here is the point. David wanted Uriah to go down to his house and to his wife Bathsheba because if Uriah went home and did the sex thing with his wife, Bathsheba, no one could ever prove that a resulting child was from David. Everyone would assume the father of Bathsheba's child would, of course, be Uriah, Bathsheba's lawful husband.

At this point David makes a terrible decision. He would simply make sure Uriah was killed in battle. And then he, David, would be free from charges of adultery and would be free to marry Bathsheba.[2]

In the morning David wrote a letter to Joab. In the letter he commanded Joab: "Set Uriah in the forefront of the hardest fighting and then draw back from him, so that he may be struck down and die."

---

1 Gehman, *New Westminster Dictionary of the Bible*, 123. BOOTH: "A rude habitation designed in most cases for a longer occupation than a tent, but not for permanence like a house. It as often formed with branches of trees."

2. In ancient Israel adultery was defined (from the male point of view) as taking another Hebraic woman. Taking a Philistine woman or any other woman taken in warfare was not considered adultery.

And so it was. Uriah was killed, just as David had planned.

When the wife of Uriah (Bathsheba) heard that her husband was dead, she made lamentation for him.

When the mourning (grieving) was over David sent and brought Bathsheba to his house, and she became his wife, and bore him a son (2 Sam 11:2–27).

Hold on! Here is the rest of the story.

2 Samuel 12:1–25:

"But the thing that David had done displeased the Lord..."

Then comes the story of the rich man and the poor man. In short, the rich man will not sacrifice one of his own lambs, but instead prevails on the poor man to kill his only beloved lamb. When David heard this story he said to Nathan: "As the Lord lives, the man who has done this *deserves to die.* (referring to the rich man.) *Thus, David has condemned himself.*

David has condemned himself through a metaphor! David, who is rich and had several other wives, tried to manipulate circumstances so that Uriah would have sex with Bathsheba and thus no one would ever know who the birth father really was.

But Nathan calls David out! "You have struck down Uriah the Hittite with the sword, and have taken his wife to be your wife; now therefore the sword shall never depart from your house, for you have despised me, and have taken the wife of Uriah the Hittite to be your wife. For you did it secretly; But I will do this thing before all Israel and before the sun."

Later, Nathan again speaks to David: "You have scorned the Lord. The child that is born to you shall die..."

"On the seventh day the child died.... Then David consoled his wife Bathsheba, and David went into her and lay with her and she bore a son and he named him Solomon..."

Chapter Twelve

Whose Reality is True?
Tests of Truth

Constructivism re-visited.
    Through these pages I have consistently held that we are the creators of our own reality. This is to say that we perceive everything outside of us to be "other" than us. Our brains are so created so as to process the results of our senses, our hearing and seeing and smelling and tasting and touching. In the process of assimilation of these five senses our brain organizes our thoughts. We learn to act, to speak, to stand erect (the vestibular or balance system) and to think. In my view, thinking is the most miraculous of our human abilities. We process the material of the senses. We have neurotransmitters that join millions of neurons together though "joiners," called synapses. When we "learn" something we can be certain that at least two neurons have connected. These neurons and synapses are kept alive by a steady flow of oxygen delivered to all parts of our body through the flow of blood being pumped by our heart.
    This brain looks out on the world and interprets to us what we think we see, feel, hear, smell, and taste. This becomes our experience of the world about us. This becomes our reality. Most of the time our realities agree with each other, although you may have a different "take" on the automobile accident or the soccer

goal than I do. "Did you see that?" I ask, as the shortstop flipped his glove in a backhand maneuver and proceeded to throw out the base runner. I could swear the ballerina was going to stumble and fall as she lept through the air into the arms of her partner.

Most of the time we see and experience these individual realities in a similar manner. This is to say we experience reality in like or similar manner. We draw similar mental pictures of what we have experienced. Until . . . we don't!

If we don't perceive things in a similar manner we try to persuade each other to see it our way. "Did you see that?" "How could you miss it?" On January 6, 2021 on T.V., I saw men and some women storming the U.S. Capitol building. You did not see what I saw? Or, if you did see what I saw, you interpreted it differently.

This difference in how we see and perceive reality leads us to ask, who is right? Who is wrong? Who is telling the truth? Who is lying? Whose set of facts are correct? Whose facts are incorrect?

Truth versus Validity

People often think: If the statement or proposition is true, it must be valid. Likewise, if a statement is valid, it must be true.

Not so! In this regard we are into the world of logic and the rules of logical thinking. Here is the basic rule. In a valid proposition we must either affirm the antecedent or we must contradict the consequent. If we contradict the antecedent or if we affirm the consequent we invalidate the proposition.

> All Democrats are liberals.
> Let us **affirm** the antecedent. John **is** a democrat.
> Therefore, **John is a liberal**.

This is a valid statement. It is also a true statement on most occasions.

Or, we could **contradict** the consequent. John is **not** a democrat.

Therefore John is **not** a liberal.

Does this mean John is a Republican?

No. This is a non-valid statement.

The point I want the reader to grasp is that validity is not a guarantor of truth. Nor is truth a guarantor of validity. A statement or proposition may be invalid and yet true. Likewise, a statement or proposition may be valid (in its logic) and yet false.

In sum, validity does not ensure truth and truth does not ensure validity.

Let us look at a well-known biblical verse about liars.

"Cretians are always liars, evil hosts, lazy gluttons." Paul is writing a letter to Titus. Titus 1:11 This biblical verse is mentioned in many philosophy books. It is called the *Cretian Paradox*.

> All Cretians are liars.
> I am a Cretian
> Therefore, I am a liar. (I have affirmed the antecedent.)

Valid. But not true.

This is valid because I have affirmed the antecedent.

What happens when I contradict the consequent?

> All Cretians are liars.
> I am **not** a liar.
> Therfore I am not a Cretian.

This is not valid because I have contradicted the consequent. I am not a liar.

> Trump supporters are skeptics about science.
> John is a Trump supporter.

This is valid because I have affirmed the antecedent. Yet it is not true.

> Trump supporters are skeptics about science.
> John is skeptical about science.
> This is not valid because I have affirmed the consequent.

And hence we come to the question of truth. Do you swear to tell the truth, the whole truth, and nothing but the truth? How do we know the truth? Whose truth is true? Whose truth is false? Are there "tests" of truth? What are they?

1. Correspondence test. This is the most common and most recognizable test of truth. Truth is the result of an agreement between the alleged facts of a situation and the observed reality. How well and to what degree does your account of truth (what really happened) correspond (agree with) my account of truth. In this manner of reasoning whatever interpretation fits or corresponds most adequately with the alleged facts of any given situation is deemed the truth. In other words, to what extent does my account of reality correspond to or agree with your account of reality?

    A prime example of correspondence theory is the January 6, 2021, insurgence upon the U.S. Capitol. Do we really know he truth of what actually happened on that afternoon? Was it an insurrection? Was it an attempted *coup d'tat*? Some witnesses say it was nothing more than a normal day. Some claim it was an invasion to interrupt the working of Congress.

2. Consensus test. Truth is the result of significant agreement among witnesses, participants, or judges. Hence, if a significant majority of people believe in the existence of god, then it must be true that there really is such a being or force. If an impressive majority of people believe in heaven or hell, then it must be so.

    What if I say, "Ninety percent of all dentists in the United States claim DENTO to be the best tooth paste on the market" does that make it so? Sixty percent of all new car dealerships in the USA prefer front wheel drive compared to rear wheel drive. So what? Does that consensus make it a fact?

    Consensus can be very dangerous. Nevertheless, consensus is the strong heart beat of the advertising industry. It is also the reality of the so-called filibuster in the U.S. Congress. Does a bill pass the House or Senate by a one point majority or does a bill require a 60 percent majority? How big a majority does it take to conclude "truth?"

Trial by Jury is a type of consensus. Each side engages lawyers who try to persuade the jurors as to what really happened.

3. Coherence test. How does my belief fit in or compare in a positive way to your belief? Does my theory of outer space cohere well with the "big bang" theory?

   Dos the theory of "parallel" universes fit in with your theory of immortality? Truth is the result of the congruence of two or more propositions or hypotheses representing diverse , yet related areas of inquiry. When independent research yields hypotheses that tend to embrace the same conclusion, it is said that the several hypotheses cohere, and that this coherence is indicative of truth.

   Do you believe in UFOs? There is still no coherence and still no consensus or correspondence about UFOs.

4. Authoritarian test. My priest tells me what is true. My minister preaches treal truth to me.

   My Congressman (or woman) tells me what is true.

5. Divine Revelation/Personal Experience. Christianity is a revealed religion. Mostly the Bible tells me what to believe. God speaks to me.

6. The STT or Semantic Theory Test of Alfred Tarski. This goes back to Aristotle. For our purpose this is a subset of correspondence theory.

7. The pragmatic theory of John Dewey.

Conclusion: truth requires an open mind. Any person who stands exclusively on one or perhaps several of the above theories or tests of truth may be in for a rude awakening. In short, there may be truth in each of them. Once we are certain that we have not confused validity with truth we may discover that truth includes several approaches to reality and therefore may best be seen as a configuration!

Chapter Thirteen

So You Want to Study the Bible!
Let's Begin with higher and Lower Criticism

HIGHER AND LOWER CRITICISM are two forms of literary criticism. When applied to the Old and New testaments (commonly called the Bible) they form the background of an academic approach to the study. First off, let us begin by pointing out that the decision as to what books should be included in the Bible, called the canon in the fourth century AD, deliberately omitted what we now call the Apocrypha, containing books that simply did not make the cut for canonical usage.

Higher or historical criticism applies to work in classical literature, art, and scripture. The task of criticism involves evaluation, relevant comparisons, and analysis. The focus of higher criticism is upon scholarship, why was it written, approximate date of the original writing, the intended audience (written to whom and for what purpose) and the location of the original writing.

Lower criticism, as contrasted with higher criticism, is textual criticism. It is a form of scholarship focusing upon the texts by rigorous examination in the light of grammar, etymology, syntax, vocabulary, phrasing, style, spelling, and sentence construction. Textual criticism may contribute to answers to questions raised by the higher criticism, especially questions of authorship and dating.

Both forms of criticism are part of the process of exegesis, the process of studying a given verse or section of Scripture, in order to expound or preach on a given text or episode (perhaps a parable or message such as the sermon on the mount). As a theological student at Princeton Seminary I had to pass both Greek and Hebrew because these were the necessary tools for exegesis and historical anthropology. I did pass, but not without agonizing struggle.

Before we consider three examples of scriptural passages that beg to be studied in depth, I wish to remind the reader that it is never enough to ask, "Isn't the Bible true?" No it is not. We have already considered the problem of truth. Let us clearly understand that the question of biblical truth must be asked sixty-six different times simply because there are sixty-six books in the Bible (thirty-nine book in the OT and twenty-seven books in the NT). To be sure, several books are written by the same author. The authorship of Luke and Acts are probably of the same pen. Also, the Pauline letters of Romans, plus 1 and 2 Corinthians have identical authorship. While most scholars agree that Paul wrote Galations and Colossians, I do not believe that Paul wrote Ephesians. Most certainly, the Pentateuch was not written by Moses.

Twelve Year Old Jesus

As illustration let us look closely at the story of twelve year old Jesus who had traveled with his parents to the temple in Jerusalem. His parents were part way home when they discovered that Jesus was not with them in their traveling retinue.

> "After three days (his parents) found him in the temple, sitting among the teachers, listening to them and asking them questions. And all who heard him were amazed at his understanding and his answers. When his parents found him they were astonished; and his mother said to him. "Child, why have you treated us like this? Look, your father and I have been searching for you in great anxiety." Luke 2:41–47.

We must ask, why is this account not recorded in the Gospels of Matthew, Mark, or John? Why is it not recorded in Q (Quelle, the source, which contains material common to Matthew and Luke but not Mark or John).[1] Why did the parents not go immediately to the Temple in their search? Did not the parents miss their son at bedtime? Or mealtime? For three days and nights? This story leaves us with many questions about parenting and perhaps discipline of children and adolescents.

> The Jesus Seminar concludes: "Both biographers and historians of the period imagined what a person would have said under the circumstances and then credited such statements to them. Luke makes extensive use of this practice, especially in the book of ACTS. At crucial points in the narrative, Luke employs language that makes events 'inevitable' or' ordained 'in accordance with some divine plan. ... This way of putting things is characteristic of Luke and appears here for the first time in his narrative."[1]

1. Funk, Hoover, *Five Gospels*, 2.

Job: Irreverent or Righteous?

A further illustration is in the last chapters (4, 7, 11) of the book of Job (referred to previously in this volume). We know because of the complete caveat I spoke about in chapter 7. At that time I said: "A complete new ending was added to Job which would forever serve to prove that Job was irreverent and way off the track of true (blind) faith. God says, "Where were you when I laid the foundation of the earth?"(38:4). Then Job recants and caves in. Of course God wins!

How do we know these chapters were added to Job? We know because they are completely at loggerheads with the rest of the book of Job. The book of Job is considered as "wisdom " literature. It simply would not do to have Job "show up" the great god of the

1. Funk, Hoover, *Five Gospels*, 15, 25–33.

universe. And so the editors conspired to have job "give in" to god. The editors fixed the race so that Job would be defeated.

The language is different. The reasoning is different. The conclusion is outrageously different. Job's wealth is restored to a degree never requested or dreamed of by Job. What began as an honest protest to god becomes a shameful reversal of plot, much like the resolution of a fairy tale. If Shakespeare did what the editors and redactors did in Job, theater buffs would have boycotted the "Bard" forever.

If we read Job, Chapter 42:21-17 we will see how, finally, the Lord god condemns Job's three well-meaning friends. Consider Job 42: 7. "After the Lord had spoken these words to Job, The Lord said to Eliphaz the Tamlnate "My wrath is kindled against you and against your two friends; for you have not spoken of me what is right, as my servant Job has." The story line now turns against Job's three friends and in favor of Job.

Job today is considered a prime example of *theodicy*, the ever-present reality of suffering, disease, and warfare. How, we must again ask, can a loving god allow the totality of pain and suffering at the hands of other humans as in warfare and also in terms of imperfect nature via nature's calamities such as earthquakes, hurricanes, floods, and human developmental and physiological and mental anomalies? (We spoke of this in Chapter Seven).

Mark's Final Verses: Mark 16:9-20

The ending of the Gospel of Mark is dubious. A discussion of Mark 14:27-31 will illustrate the exegetical problems.[2] The ending of the book of Mark is an example of editorial redaction and additional verbiage. Authorities (RSV, NTSV, and even the more conservative King James Version ends Mark at 16:8.) My *New International Version* of King James states at the end of 16:8 "The most reliable

---

2. Funk, Hoover, *Five Gospels*, 127. "Once again we find words attributed to Jesus indirectly. In Mark 16:7 the youth in a white robe, who appears at the tomb, instructs the women to go and tell the disciples that Jesus is going to Galilee and 'there they will see him' just as he told you."

early manuscripts and other Greek witnesses do not have Mark 16:9–20." *Not all renditions of the King James version (original date: 1611) share this important disclaimer.* In fact, the end of Mark has become one of the most powerful literary foundations for belief in the resurrection of Jesus. I simply cannot believe in the resurrection account of Jesus when it is based on Mark 16:9–20.

Mark 16:9–20 contains material on Mary Magdalene, Jesus appearing to his disciples, Jesus' commission to his disciples, and ends with Jesus' ascension into heaven. Mark 16:9–20 is widely considered to be an added ending to satisfy early skeptics regarding the alleged resurrection of Jesus from the dead.

In conclusion, I can only wish that serious students of the Bible would go online and invest money in credible biblical commentaries such as the *Interpreters Bible,* the *Abingdon Bible Commentary,* the *Westminster Dictionary of the Bible,* and the *Five Gospels.*

CHAPTER FOURTEEN

Credulous and Incredulous

CREDULOUS AND INCREDULOUS: CREDULITY and incredulity. Why do people believe? Why do people not believe, regardless of the subject or object of belief?

Why do some believe in god? Why do some scoff at the god hypothesis? Why do some people believe intently in COVID-19 vaccinations? Why do some people believe strongly against COVID-19 vaccinations? Why does Donald Trump believe he won the 2020 American presidential election? Why does Donald Trump not believe he was defeated? Why do over 30 percent of adult Americans eligible for the COVID-19 vaccines, as of this writing, remain unvaccinated?

Why? Why? Why?

Is it class structure?

Is it blue collar or white collar or sweaty fatigues?

Is it income stratification?

Is it parental status?

Is it our parents?

Is it our family?

Is it type of work?

Is it brawn work or brain work?

Is it level of public education?

Is it level of post-high school education?

Is it status and prestige of one's college or university?

Is it one's neighborhood?

Is it one's section of town or city?

Is it one's vehicle or other means of transport?

Is it political party or persuasion?

Is it rural or urban?

Is it religious faith?

Or lack thereof?

Is it suburbs or hi-rises?

Is it people of color?

Is it degree of whiteness?

Is it prejudice against science?

Is it perceived level of sophistication?

Is it perceived level of knowledge?

Is it perceived level of *oxi authentikos*?

It is all of these things!

Do we need help from sociologists and psychologists? Or is there already a strong mindset against the highly educated and the highly credentialed?

In short, why do we believe whatever it is we believe? How do we learn or acquire our beliefs? How do we know what we think we know? In a manner of speaking, this is a question of personal epistemology.

This chapter is built on certain presuppositions.

1. Everything we know or claim to know is based on some kind of learning. We begin to learn at birth. Consider how quickly a neonate learns to "root" for the breast.

2. Everything we fear is based on both learning and experience. If we did not learn to fear heights we would not survive. Fear of the unknown is a basic cause for belief about life after death.

3. Almost everything the masses believe in terms of religious faith is "revealed" truth, not based on reason or scientific inquiry. Fear of the results of scientific inquiry, in itself, is reason for many people's resistance to vaccinations, be it smallpox or COVID-19.

4. Doubting and skeptical reasoning are our cognitive friends. Learning to doubt many claims to truth keeps us from foolish behaviors such as eating all kinds of foods we have learned are not good for us. Humankind appeared to want to believe that smoking tobacco products was not harmful to the human body. Today people have come to defend vaping and electric cigarettes in spite of evidence of potential harm to the body.

5. Misinformation always has a payoff for the misinformers. Follow the rewards for disbelief. Who profits and how? Political parties and lawmakers often have much to gain by spreading untruth. Foremost in potential payoff for political party allegiance by elected officials, from city councils to county and school board members, is reelection.

But still?

Why the Jan 6 resurgence?

Why the naysayers regarding the COVID vaccine?

Why the stonewalling by the Republicans?

Why does McConnell do the McConnell dance?

Why does Lindsey Graham do the Lindsey dance?

Why do people seem to believe what they want most to believe? Or wish to be true?

Why do people turn against science?

Why does the public voice renounce science?

Not to mention:

Why does Trump lie, steal, provoke, accuse?

The roots of our beliefs.

Our beliefs reflect our insecurity, our anxiety, our fear, and our personal failures. What a person believes defines him or her. It marks him or her as having a unique perspective on life. Joan Williams, in her remarkable sociological best seller, *White Working Class: Overcoming Class Cluelessness in America*, makes this statement of note:

> "Understanding working class resentment of the poor needs to begin by looking at everyday life for working-class Americans of all ages."[1]

Williams defines Americans who are in the middle class as working class.

> "I had a lively discussion with my editor about what to call various groups in this book. I wanted to call the group in the middle the middle class, well, because *they are*. My editor wisely pointed out that racists would be confused by that, if middle class is a term that we all use to describe ourselves regardless of whether it reflects reality. So I agreed to call those Americans in the middle—the ones who are neither rich nor poor—the "working class". But, as part of the deal, I got to refer to the people at the top as an "elite." ...Who composes this group? Americans with household incomes in the top 20% and at least one member who is a college graduate. The 2015 medium income of such families was $173,175.00. Roughly 16.5 % of American households fit this definition of the professional-marginal elite (PME)." [1]
>
> 1. Williams, *White Working Class*, 10.

1. Williams, *White Working Class*, 14.

CREDULOUS AND INCREDULOUS

Williams calls the people at the top of the elite working class the professional marginal elite (PME). I think this is misleading. I much prefer to center my remarks about class around the "haves" and the "have-nots". I say this not as a sociologist but rather as a "have-not" lower class minister (three pastorates, 1956–67).

Even in that time period there seemed to be a generalized "armed truce" between people without means and people with means. The first two of these pastorates (Saginaw, Michigan and Battle Creek, Michigan) saw an alliance between Democrats and Republicans with a strong central leader who had a knack for helping folks feel good about themselves. Both the "have-nots" and the "haves" liked Dwight Eisenhower. Then came Kennedy and the long nightmare of assassination. The Battle Creek experience was a lesson for me as to how to relate and not relate to "have-nots"). And now, in a village near Syracuse, I was living and working more among the "haves." (I was a pastor in a "have" church near Syracuse, New York). Later, in the eighties even Ronald Reagan seemed to help the have-nots feel better about themselves and about life in general. (When Reagan said "The problem is government" he made countless thousands very happy. And yet this statement was quite an empty effort to soothe ruffled feathers and make people feel good about their prejudices.)

Here follows a dangerous generalization. In hindsight, have-nots seemed less happy and contented than haves. Have-nots seemed resentful of those who were better off. They were also more forgiving and accepting of the "haves".[2]

In the present era of Trump we live in a time when the have-nots have latched onto a tribal leader who speaks to them and values them and will go to extremes in order to demonstrate that support. Trump demonstrates this by the way he talks down to

---

2. The separation of thee "haves" from the "have nots" is best illustrated when the ambivalent "middle" is eliminated from data analysis. Think back to test taking in high school. Nobody wanted to get a B with 89 percent compared to an A with 90 percent. Students with 89 percent felt cheated! Was there really that much difference between 89 and 90? The wider the gap between the two extremes of haves and have-nots simply allows us to see more clearly and emphatically the differences between the two extremes.

people he wishes to denigrate and by the way he personally relates to his own sexuality (*Hollywood Access* tape) and by the way he shows a fearless superiority to fellow "haves" and tribal members.

Trump plays to the have-nots. He despises science, the arts, and the classics. Trump thrives on the resentment of the have-nots to the point that the have-nots will go to any length to prove their loyalty to their leader. Truth is of no importance to have- nots. Nor is integrity. Or science. For the religious have-nots, the increasing numbers of evangelical and fundamentalist Christians who disdain abortion and biblical criticism of any kind, the Trumpian stand against abortion is fuel for the soul and proof enough of Trump's legitimacy to power.

The most surprising result of the January 6, 2021 insurrection against the Capitol is the staunch denial by elected Republican senators and representatives of the reality of the insurrection or coup attempt. Rest assured, it was a coup attempt with Trump heralding his own reinstatement, claiming the results of the November 2020 presidential election to be a lie and his re-installation a matter of time.

To most Americans, it is incredulous how Trump passes off his lies. He pretends to be credulous (he believes) that the majority of voters voted for him, although no fraudulent votes or voter schemes have been uncovered. It appears people will cling stubbornly to what they believe in spite of reason and evidence (or lack thereof). The Trumpian big lie is a sedative wherein good, decent, mostly law-abiding citizens feel they have been heard! This is sheer demagoguery. Why do people believe this cascade of lies and filth? Because it make them feel better, if only until the next Fox newscast featuring Tucker Carlson.

Again, why are many of the have-nots incredulous as to the significance of the COVID-19 vaccines? Why are people accepting (or appearing to accept) the put-down by Trump followers regarding Anthony Fauci? To me this is incredulous. I accept Fauci as a voice of science, fallible (yes, we all are) committed to the scientific method and its credulous and rigorous standards.

Anthony Fauci represents the best of scientific research. He is credulous. Trump, on the other hand, appears to me to be absolutely incredulous. He makes outrageous statements and when he does not know what else to say he engages in an *ad hominem* (to the person) attack on his opponent (a tactic we all learned in junior high school or earlier).

Trump is a cry baby. He knows what he is doing. He simply repeats the lies and the accusations *ad nausea* and with such force and affected innocence that his would be "have-not" followers feel better about themselves, their situations, and their place within their tribal social order. Napoleon would be proud. Hitler and his Nazi co-conspirators would be elated.

In sum, the pay-off for the have-nots is an increased positive feeling about themselves and about life. They feel better, but at what price? This is tragic.

Scientific Methodology: Putting Doubt and Skepticism to Good Use

One of the most reliable and irreplaceable tenets of the scientific method is the principle held forth by Carl Popper, the principle of falsifiability. If a tenet or belief is ever held to be unfalsifiable it cannot and will not be credited with absolute truth.[3]

I personally grieve when I hear people renounce the COVID vaccines. What did they learn in high school or junior high about the scientific method? Just this morning I heard a news report of a male preacher shouting out that nobody with a mask would be permitted in his (?) church building. Where, when, and how did this "man of god" learn this godfoolery nonsense?

Let us look at the falsification principle of Karl Popper. Basically, Popper is saying that if a so-called scientific finding cannot be falsified, it is not a scientific finding or theory. In order for science

---

3. *Oxford Dictionary of Philosophy*, s.v. "Karl Popper," 135–36.

to be science there must be an ongoing possibility of rejection.[4] It is in this sense that science is the child of doubt and skepticism.

At this writing the three vaccines for COVID-19 stand at the 99.99 percent level of protection, at the .001 level and none have been falsified. What does this mean?

Stated negatively, if something cannot be falsified or demonstrated to be false then it not only cannot be stated as true, it cannot be called science or scientific theory.

Statisticians and research statistics, especially in psychology and the social sciences, use "levels of significance" as means of measurement. If a research conclusion is statistically significant at the .05 level of significance it means there are five chances out of one hundred chances of getting these results by *chance alone*. However, in most studies verification need not be absolutely 100 percent. If a result is significant at the .01 level of significance it means there is only one chance out of one hundred of getting these results by *chance alone*.[5]

Popper insisted that positive verification was not enough to establish a theory. In other words the null hypotheses must be rejected. Then, by recreating and retesting the null repeatedly using different language and assumptions, scientific theory is established. The key difference is that Popper refused to accept the word, *verification* as having scientific authority. Popper accepts and utilizes the word and concept of corroboration. Rejection of null hypotheses as a result of testing for falsification is, according to Popper, a far more promising avenue to scientific corroboration and discovery than the concept of verification based on statistical significance.

---

4. *Oxford Dictionary of Philosophy*, s.v. "Karl Popper," 135–36.

5. Some may say, "So what? What does he know?" In December of 2020, Marjorie, my wife, and I were both hospitalized with COVID-19. Marjorie died of COVID-19/pneumonia. I recovered. A month later I had the first of two COVID shots. We were both in our ninetieth year.

"Sir Karl Popper(1902–94) considered one of the most influential philosophers of science, asserted that for a theory to be science, a necessary condition is that the theory consist of hypotheses that could be falsified. According to Popper falsification is the best approach for testing scientific theories and contrasts sharply with the verification approach. The theory must be organized in a way such that its assertions can be refuted. This necessity for a scientific theory to be falsifiable is known as *demarcation criterion*. Advocating the use of falsifiability as a scientific method to test theories, Popper therefore rejected inductivism, because falsification dictates that you must begin with falsifiable hypotheses before observations are made. Then you collect data to refute them, not verify them."[1]

1. Crosby, DiClemente, Salazaar, *Research Methods In Health Promotion*, 37–38.

Most null hypotheses are simply the negative of the proposition being tested. For Popper this is not enough. True establishment of a theory may depend upon repeated attempts to falsify the major premises of the theory. When repeated falsification fails, the theory may stand until repeated failures point to the fact that the theory is no longer supported by research. Or, ongoing and continuing research and hypothesis testing may serve as corroborating evidence (not verification) as to the first hand accuracy of the continuing hypotheses based on falsification theory.[6]

So You Wish to Reject Vaccination

Go Ahead. Listen to the Proud Boys and all the other Capitol insurrectionists who stormed the Capitol, defecated in the hallways and acted like little children protesting the teachings of their master. Go ahead and endanger yourself and your wife or husband and your precious children. Pit yourself against science . . . and research experts like Anthony Fauci and all the disease control centers of the world. At this writing we are over five million dead. Good luck. I'll be thinking of you!

6. *Stanford Encyclopedia*, "Karl Popper."

CHAPTER FIFTEEN

Death

An Existential Paradox

FIRST WE MUST NOTE that purpose in life is not necessarily the same as meaning in life. One may identify several or many purposes that weave in and out of one's daily existence. Yet herein I raise the greater existential question of an overall purpose or meaning of one's being. I suggest that death is a paradox. How can death be integral to the meaning of life and yet be the final exit point of life? A paradox refers to two things, items, or events that exclude each other. Can death be both?

Regarding purpose I turn to Viktor Frankl and his explanation of *Logotherapy*.[1]

Framed in this manner, the question I raise is whether or not, and in what sense, the fact of death, in itself, gives meaning to life.

I frame this question as a paradox in that death itself is the cessation of biological life. The heart stops beating. Blood carrying oxygen stops circulating and the lungs no longer carry blood to the brain and to the thousands and thousands of outlets and capillaries throughout our bodies.

So how can death, thus defined, give meaning to human existence?

---

1. Frankl, *Man's Search For Meaning*. Published originally as "Saying yes to life: A psychologist experiences the concentration camp."

Death

I believe that a *configuration* of purpose, wherein there is harmonious resolution of conflict, does yield a deeper and more complete meaning of one's existence. A configuration refers to a scheme or pattern of values wherein each value fits well with the other values without conflict, much like the interlocking pieces of a puzzle.

The answer is both simple and profound. Death gives meaning to life because it brings to a definitive end the days, months, and years of life.

However, death, paradoxically, does not, in itself, give meaning to life, but rather death creates an end-time or end-event that forever prevents the individual from seeking and fulfilling the immediate purposes of his/her existence. Death is thus the cut-off point after which there is no possibility of purposeful fulfillment or accomplishment.

Without an end point there can be no meaning to everyday existence as experienced by the individual. This is the basic meaning of existentialism. As such, it is the basic meaning of death. If there were no end to life there could be no purposeful fulfillment of any and all human endeavors. There could, however, be meaning of the deceased person's life in the memory of survivors, i.e. relatives, and of course immediate nuclear and extended family.

Think of what would happen if the end of any sporting event were summarily erased or postponed...perhaps into an endless series of overtimes, matches, quarters, penalty kicks, periods or what-have-you extensions. There could simply be no end to the event. Or consider a chess tournament, a bridge contest, or a musical contest between harp players without do-overs. *Without a well-defined end-point there simply can be no meaning to the event.*

Is death the meaning of life (or existence?)

Or does death contribute to the meaning of life (or existence)?

Without death would (or could) there be meaning to human existence as experienced by the individual?

Without death what would be (or could be) the point of living?

Would the world's religions exist if there were no death?

If there were no death would there be such a thing as morality or ethics?

If there were no death what would be the capacity of the earth to support the expanding population in terms of food, sustenance, and income?

Our use of language is very important. Let us decide to lay aside the word "death". Let us substitute the word "finis" or even finish. Life as we know it ends at the finis, the finish line, or at the end point.

We now re-address the question. What is the meaning of finis? What does it mean to have a finis to any event or endeavor? Does the end or finis or finish give meaning to the event? If yes, then we must assess the usage and the importance of the concept of "finis".

For many practitioners of existentialism the over-worked question, "Does essence precede existence or does existence precede essence?" has served as an introduction to philosophical enquiry (essence usually defined as "logos" or meaning/purpose).

Does human life have a pre-given meaning or set of purposes prior to physiological conception and birth or does meaning and purpose result from the living of this life? The existentialist sees meaning as the resulting product and byproduct of living in all of its dimensions.

Commitments to providential meaning and the theological tenets of many persuasions hypothesize religious and philosophical belief with claims that divinity or divine revelation secures for humanity a pre-given meaning to all existence.[2] Thus, some sort of divine revelation enters our existence even before are born. In contrast to divine revelation I think of existentialists such as Camus, Sartre, Kierkegaard, and Kafka. For these existentialist thinkers, existence precedes essence! First comes life. Then comes the meaning we give to our life.

Let us rephrase several questions and phrases.

---

2. Consider the Pentateuch, the New Testament, the Calvinistic *Westminster Confession of Faith*, and the *Koran*.

Is death the meaning of life? (Or existence.)

Or does death *contribute* to the meaning of life? (Or existence)

Without death would (or could) there be meaning to human existence as experienced by the individual?

Without death what would be (or could be) the point of living?

Would the world's religions exist if there were no death?

Is religion a response to life or is religion a response to death?

If there were no death would there be such a thing as morality?

If there were no death what would be the capacity of the earth to support the expanding total population in terms of food, sustenance, and income?

Our use of language here is very important. Let us decide to lay aside the word "death". Let us substitute the word "finis" or even "finish". Life as we know it ends at the finis, the finish line, or at the end.

We must rephrase our question. What is the meaning of finis? What does it mean to have a finish to any event or endeavor? Does the end or finis or finish give meaning to the event? If yes, then we must assess the usage and importance of the concept of "finis".

Proposition

Here is my proposition: Any event that entails a finite ending draws its meaning, at least in part, from the reality that there is a definite ending, an end point or absolute conclusion. *So I invite the reader to join with me in thinking of death as the finis, the end game of personal existence.*

In this enquiry concerning death and the meaning of life I shall continue the discussion by beginning with the prison experience of Viktor Frankl and then turn to the prison experience of Dietrich Bonhoeffer and the existential premise that we are the meaning-givers.[3] Space prohibits me from discussion of Rollo May,

---

3. Bonhoeffer, *Letters and Papers From Prison*, 5–6.

Erich Fromm, Karen Horney, and Paul Tillich, each of whom, in their own way, speaks to the existentialist premise that we are the meaning-givers and that we do the dance of meaning while we go through this unique lifetime.[4]

Viktor Frankl

Viktor Frankl was a psychiatrist who somehow escaped the death chamber. His survival from the brutalities of Auschwitz remains as a monument to the horrors of the Nazi regime and to the power of the human brain to persist in the midst of total chaos.

> The way in which a man accepts his fate and all the suffering it entails, the way in which he takes up his cross, gives him ample opportunity—even under the most difficult circumstances—to add a deeper meaning to his life. It may remain brave, dignified and unselfish. Or, in the bitter fight for self-preservation he may forget his human dignity and become no more than an animal. Here lies the chance for a man either to make use of or to forgo the opportunities of attaining the moral values that a difficult situation may afford him. And this decides whether he is worthy of his sufferings or not. ... New arrivals usually knew nothing about the conditions of a camp. Those who had come back from other camps were obliged to keep silent, and from some camps no one had returned. On entering camp a change took place in the minds of the men. With the end of uncertainty there came the uncertainty of the end. It was impossible to forsee whether or when, if at all, this form of existence would end.[1]
>
> 1. Frankl, Man's Search for Meaning, 63–64.

Frankl believed that life expected meaning and purpose from the living. "We had to learn ourselves and, furthermore, we had to teach the despairing men, that *it did not really matter what we expected from life, but rather what life expected from us.* We needed to stop asking about the meaning of life, and instead to think of

---

4. Tillich, *Courage To Be.* Horney, *Neurotic Personality of Our Time.* Fromm, *Man For Himself.* May, *Man's Search For Himself.*

ourselves as those who were being questioned by life—daily and hourly. Our answer must consist, not in talk about meditation, but in right action and in right conduct. Life ultimately means taking the responsibility to find the right answers to its problems and to fulfill the tasks which it constantly sets for each individual."[5]

Dietrich Bonhoeffer

I next consider Dietrich Bonhoeffer. Bonhoeffer did not have to return to Germany. He could have remained in the United States at Union Theological Seminary in New York City as an exchange guest faculty. However, he believed fervently that he should return to his own people in Germany during their worsening travail. He was eventually accused of being involved in an assassination plot against Hitler and he was hanged on April 9, 1945, just one month before the German surrender.

Frankl lived and wrote from the psychiatric and psychological points of view whereas Bonhoeffer thought and wrote from a theological point of view. Yet, although their prime reference points were quite divergent, their respective responses were much the same. Nevertheless, there was a profound difference. Whereas Frankl was a prisoner amongst numberless other prisoners, daily fighting for their very existence amongst Jews, gypsies, and other political unwanteds, Bonhoeffer was a political prisoner awaiting trial for alleged acts against the Nazi regime via his role in the Confessional Church of Germany.

In his *Letters and Papers From Prison* Bonhoeffer reveals himself to be primarily a thoroughgoing disciple of Jesus Christ.[6] Bonhoeffer was, in theological terms, a conservative Lutheran pastor and theologian. In terms of "atonement" theory, Bonhoeffer believed that Jesus was the Son of God, the Word become flesh who gave himself for the redemption of those who confess him as Lord and Savior. He embraced what is described by theologians

---

5. Frankl, *Man's Search For Meaning*, 72.
6. See especially *Cost of Discipleship*, and *Life Togeth*er.

as penal substitution, Christus Victor, ransom, and satisfaction theories, while holding strongly to examplar ethics. There is little in Bonhoeffer to cause us to sense an internal struggle with doubt or unbelief. In short, Bonhoeffer was steadfast in his belief, i.e. that he belonged to Jesus who is called the Christ.

> *Irina Ratushinskaya, in the Introduction to the SCM edition of* Letters and Papers from Prison *writes:*
>
> > The letters are not the letters of some super-hero on a pedestal, but those of a real person, who froze, ailed, needed handerkerchiefs, was happy to receive parcels from home, missed his finance,' dreamed of freedom and prayed for it. He prayed for his gaolers too. He was able to correlate all these things. This is probably why, from his prison cell, he was able to write in such a way as to help anyone, especially in times of difficulty and loneliness, to feel hopeful.

In Bonhoeffer's view death was emphatically *not* the meaning of life. He lived his life in the shadow of hope and limitless trust. If anything, hope kept him alive and well. We do not know, we cannot know, what effect the possibility of approaching death had upon him. He had nothing else to hold onto. How Bonhoeffer approached his final days remains an inspiration for all humankind, believers and non-believers alike.

Bonhoeffer said quite clearly: "In these turbulent times we repeatedly lose sight of what really makes life worth living. We think that. because this or that person is living, it makes sense for us to live too. But the truth is that if this earth was good enough for the man Jesus Christ, if such a man as Jesus lived, *then, and only then, has life a meaning for us.* (Italics added) If Jesus had not lived then our life would be meaningless, in spite of all the other people whom we know and honour and love...the unbiblical idea of 'meaning' is indeed only a translation of what the Bible calls 'promise.'"[7]

---

7. Bonhoeffer, *Letters and Papers From Prison*, 348.

Death

A Final Caveat

To this point we have been thinking about death as a singular event. In truth, the death event does not, in itself, give meaning to life. What gives meaning to life is the inescapable fact that homo sapiens, (dating from circa seventy thousand years ago) to the best of our knowledge, is the only creature in all known creation that can contemplate her/his own demise.[8]

While Bonhoeffer was preoccupied with his forthcoming trial by the Nazi's and the injustice of his imprisonment, Frankl was daily fighting for his personal survival. To Frankl, death was the utter and absolute cessation of human existence. To Bonhoeffer death was but a transition from the realm of human existence to reunion with Christ in his glory.

The heart of the issue is not death itself, but my death and your death. Put another way, it is not the reality of the death event itself but the reality of *my* death that stands central to the question of the meaning of death. How does my knowledge of the fact of my own death affect me now?

Thus framed, does the reality of my own forthcoming death give meaning to my existence? I answer without equivocation: yes.

The meaning of death to me entails such total finality that not a single word can be added or subtracted, a single deed or action added or subtracted, or a single reprise reenacted or repeated. Death is the Final Take. The meaning of my existence is in the fact that I cannot redo or redirect (or redo the choreography) of a single note or a single decision.[9]

In sum:

Frankl left us with a method of psychotherapy structurally connected to self-examination and attitude toward life whereas

---

8. Harari, *Sapiens*, 15. Other sources estimate Sapiens from fifty thousand to thirty thousand years ago.

9. It is in this sense that death can be better compared to a stage play than to a movie or motion picture. In the midst of a performance the stage play cannot be stopped and re-scripted. The motion picture can only be re-scripted on the cutting room floor under director supervision.

Bonhoeffer left us an example of faith in eternal discipleship to the Son of God.

Bonhoeffer was not at all concerned with the meaning of death apart from union with God and Jesus. Bonhoeffer embraced the "Christ" event as postulated by Karl Barth and the Confessing Church of Germany. On the other hand, Frankl was himself a human exemplar for the facing of life in the midst of death within the horrible confines of the concentration camp.

Bibliography

Becker, Ernest. *The Denial of Death*. New York: Macmillan, 1973.
Bonhoeffer, Dietrich. *Letters and Papers from Prison*. New York: Touchstone, 1997.
Boston, Robert. *Taking Liberties: Why Religious Freedom Doesn't Give You the Right To Tell Other People What To Do*. Buffalo: Prometheus, 2014.
Brody, B. "Fetal Humanity and the Theory of Essentials." In *Philosophy and Sex*, edited by Robert Baker and Frederick Elliston. Buffalo: Prometheus, 1975.
Bushnell, Horace. *Nature and the Supernatural: As Together Constituting The One System of God*. London: Forgotten, 1858.
Calvin, John. *The Institutes of the Christian Religion*. Translated by Henry Beveridge. Peabody, MA: Hendrickson, 2008.
Church, Forrest. *Love and Death: My Journey Through the Valley of the Shadow*. Boston: Beacon. 2008.
Coleridge, Samuel Taylor. *The Rime of the Ancient Mariner*. New York: Dover, 1970.
Crosby, John Fulling. *Faithlore: The Invented Reality*. Eugene, OR: Wipf and Stock, 2018.
———. *Sons and Fathers: Challenges To Paternal Authority*. London: Routledge, 2014.
———. *Aftermath: Surviving the Loss of God*. New York: Algora, 2013.
———. *The Flipside of Godspeak: Theism As Constructed Reality*. Eugene, OR. Wipf and Stock, 2007.
———. "When Does Human Life Begin?" *American Journal of Orthopsychiatry*. American Orthopsychiatric Association. April, 1980
Crosby, Richard A., DiClemente, Ralph, Salazaar, Laura. *Research Methods In Health Promotion*. San Francisco: John Wiley and Sons, 2006.
Epstein, Greg. *Good Without God: What a Billion Nonreligious People Do Believe*. New York: Harper and Collins, 2009.
Ehrman, Bart D. *Did Jesus Exist? The Historical Argument For Jesus of Nazareth*. New York: Harper Collins, 2012.
———. *Jesus Interrupted: Revealing the Hidden Contradictions In the Bible*. New York: Harper Collins, 2009.

Bibliography

———. *God's Problem: How the Bible Fails to Answer Our Most Important Question—Why We Suffer*. New York: Harper Collins, 2008.

———. *Lost Christianities: The Battles For Scripture and the Faiths We Never Knew*. New York: Oxford University Press, 2003.

———. *Jesus: Apocalyptic Prophet of the New Millenium*. New York: Oxford University Press, 1999.

Etherington, Lucy. "Melanie Klein and Object Relations Theory." *Psychology Today*, February 12, 2020.

Frankl, Viktor E. *Man's Search For Meaning*. Boston, Beacon, 1958.

Freud, Sigmund. *The future of An Illusion*. New York: Liveright, 1957.

Fromm, Erich. *Man For Himself*. New York: Random House, 1947

Funk, Robert W. *The Gospel of Jesus: According to the Jesus Seminar*. Santa Rosa: Polebridge, 1999.

Funk, Robert W. and Roy W. Hoover. *The Five Gospels: What Did Jesus Really Say?* San Francisco: Harper, 1993.

Hardin, G. "Abortion or compulsory pregnancy?" *Journal of Marriage and the Family*. 30.2 (1968) 246.

Horney, Karen. *The Neurotic Personality of Our Time*. New York: W. W. Norton, 1937.

Gehman, Henry Snyder. *The New Westminster Dictionary of the Bible*. Philadelphia: Westminster, 1976.

Grinsead, J.W. *A Short History of the Doctrine of the Atonement*. London: Manchester University Press, 1970.

Harari, Yuval Noah. *Sapiens: A Brief History of Mankind*. New York: Harper Collins, 2015.

Hepp, Maylon H. *Reflective Thinking*. Granville, OH: Denison University, 1950–51.

Hume, David. *Dialogues Concerning Natural Religion*. New York: Barnes and Noble, 2006.

Jaggar, A. "A Woman's Right To Decide." *Philos Forum* 5.1–2 (1973) 347–360.

Kendi, Ibran X. *Stamped From the Beginning: The Definitive History of Racist Ideas In America*. New York: Hatcher, 2017.

Maslin, Mark. *Climate Change*. Oxford: Oxford University Press.

May, Rollo. *Man's Search For Himself*. New York: W. W. Norton, 1953.

Meacham, Jon. *His Truth Is Marching On: John Lewis and the Power of Hope*. New York: Random House.

Newby, Ron. *Tribalism: An Existential Threat To Humanity*. New York: Lulu, 2020.

Nuland, Sherwin B. *How We Die: Reflections On Life's final Chapter*. New York: Random House, 1995.

Oxford Dictionary of Philosophy. Edited by Simon Blackburn. Oxford: Oxford University Press, 2016.

Packer, George. "A New Report Offers Insights into Tribalism in the Age of Trump." *The New Yorker*, May 4, 2021.

BIBLIOGRAPHY

Rahmeier, P. "Abortion and the reverence for life." *Christian Century*, May 1971.

Schweitzer, Albert. *The Quest of the Historical Jesus. A Critical Study of its Progress from Reimarus to Wrede*. London: A. C. Black, 1911.

Sahakian and Sahakian, *Ideas of the Great Philosophers*. New York: Harper Collins, 2005.

Spong, John Shelby. *Biblical Literalism: A Gentile Heresy*. New York: Harper Collins, 2016.

Saslow, Eli, *Rising Out of Hatred: The Awakening of a Former White Nationalist*. New York: Random House, 2018.

Strauss, David Friedrich. *The Life of Jesus Critically Examined*. New York: Macmillan, 1892.

Thompson, J. "A defense of abortion." *Philos* 1.1 (1971) 47–66.

Tillich, Paul. *The Courage To Be*. New Haven: Yale University Press, 1952.

Von Glasersfeld, Ernest. *Radical Constructivism: A Way of Knowing and Learning*. London and New York: Routledge, 1995.

Watzlawick, Paul. *The Invented Reality: Conributions To Consructivism*. New York: Norton, 1984.

Wilkerson, Isabel. *Caste: The Origins of our Discontents*. New York: Random House, 2020.

Williams, Joan. *White Working Class: Overcoming Class Cluelessness in America*. Boston: Harvard Business Review Press, 2020.

Younger, Sabastian. *Tribe: On Homecoming and Belonging*. New York: Twelve, 2016.

www.ingramcontent.com/pod-product-compliance
Lightning Source LLC
Chambersburg PA
CBHW070325100426
42743CB00011B/2562